COLONIAL FAMILIES OF

SURRY

AND

ISLE OF WIGHT COUNTIES, VIRGINIA

VOLUME 5

ISLE OF WIGHT COUNTY, VIRGINIA
DEEDS, WILLS, CONVEYANCES
BOOK A

1628–1659

Compiled by
JOHN ANDERSON BRAYTON

HERITAGE BOOKS
2025

HERITAGE BOOKS

AN IMPRINT OF HERITAGE BOOKS, INC.

Books, CDs, and more—Worldwide

For our listing of thousands of titles see our website
at
www.HeritageBooks.com

A Facsimile Reprint
Published 2025 by
HERITAGE BOOKS, INC.
Publishing Division
5810 Ruatan Street
Berwyn Heights, MD 20740

First printing, 2001, Jackson, Mississippi
Second printing, 2014, Baltimore, Maryland

Library of Congress Control Number 2014953668

International Standard Book Number
Paperbound: 978-0-7884-5074-7

TABLE OF CONTENTS

INTRODUCTION AND ACKNOWLEDGEMENTS

Never quite content with the information contained in even the most assiduously prepared abstracts, and secretly (and perversely) convinced that some wildly important piece of information has escaped the intrepid abstracter's eye, I offer an "infallible" solution. Volume three of this series contained a verbatim transcript of the Isle of Wight Co., VA, late seventeenth century Court Orders. Volume five, herein, contains a verbatim transcript of the book of Isle of Wight County's oldest records—Book A, Deeds, Will, Conveyances, taken from the Library of Virginia microfilm so labeled, followed by the dates "1636-1767." The year 1767 refers, of course, to the Isle of Wight Co., VA, Guardian Account records, which commence in 1740 and end in 1767. What the date "1636" indicates, or why it is part of Book A's title, is a mystery.

The earliest record contained in Book A is in reality dated 19 Oct 1628, and the latest 2 Aug 1659. A transcript made from the microfilm, parts of which were illegible, was checked against and corrected from the volume at the Isle of Wight Co., VA, Courthouse at Isle of Wight, VA. I am aware that abstracts of this record book exist, but I feel that readers will enjoy the style of the recopied, whole text. Unfortunately, Book A itself does not date from 1628; it was, as explained on its first page, recopied from loose papers found in the courthouse by scribe James Baker in 1733. So the script is only eighteenth century, not early seventeenth.

Therefore, I have reproduced the script as carefully as I could, even though it is not representative of the original loose records, which I assume have been destroyed. James Baker had a habit of mixing his abbreviations and upper-case letters, but his script is clear and easy to read. This indicates that the earlier records which he copied were more than likely in a fair state of preservation. There are very few gaps in Mr. Baker's renditions.

I have every intention of transcribing Will & Deed Books 1 and 2, in their entireties, at some point in the near future. This will place into the hands of anyone who wants it nearly *all* of Isle of Wight's extant seventeenth century records.[1] The Henrico Co., VA, series of abstracts, instituted by the venerable Dr. Weisiger, are of course ground-breaking in their genealogical importance for the Henrico—Chesterfield area. But the

---

[1] It remains to be seen if, after completing the two Will & Deed Books, I really need to transcribe Deed Book 1. As of this moment, I have transcribed more than ¾ of Will & Deed Book 1.

division of the original records into simply wills or deeds has left out a great deal of important information which the genealogical public does not presently have. For instance, the abstracts of Isle of Wight County, VA, Will & Deed Book 1, found unpaginated in John Bennett Boddie's *Seventeenth Century Isle of Wight*, were not included in William Lyndsay Hopkins's abstracts of Isle of Wight Co. early deeds; and many of the incidental records were left out of both versions. As a case in point, the Orphans' Court records of Will & Deed Book 2 have never seen the light of day. This is a shame. They are essential to early Isle of Wight Co., VA, research. Boddie was exceedingly "terse" in his abstracts of some of the court depositions in these records, for reasons, I would assume, of their earthy contents—they are some of the most interesting testimonials in seventeenth century Virginia history, and certainly some of the most entertaining. This transcriber plans to omit nothing.

I hope that this will serve as an example to other abstracters to cease the practice of reproducing only portions of the record books which they are abstracting. The easy availability of abstracts of all varieties—about which this researcher is nevertheless delighted—tends to make one gradually assume that, for an inaccessible Virginia county, a half-baked loaf is better than no bread at all.

One has only to read the will of testator John Moon in its entirety to get a flavor of the early piety and religious fervor which must have been a constant in the life of the earliest colonists. On the other hand, these records are a lesson in the gradual transformation of the legal system as it developed from English common law into a language that was distinctly Virginian.

A word about the dating system: Regnal years abound in these records, but one must remember that Charles I reigned only 23 full years and 10 months into his 24th. Any years referring to regnal years after that must be assumed to refer to the first years of the Commonwealth, which must not have had much meaning for the colonies, in terms of their dating system.

I have arranged the documents in the text chronologically on the following page, just for pure entertainment. Dates of documents which are enclosed in brackets were simply not dated in the text, and the bracketed date is that of its recording.

In many ways, this is a work of pure indulgence; but, it is also a beginning. I have the following persons to thank for their encouragement: Dr. Edgar MacDonald and Mr. Robert Young Clay of Richmond, VA; Mr. Trent Roberts of Detroit, MI; and Lucky, Catfish, Moose, and Jinx.

Chronological arrangement of the instruments within:

Date	Item #	Instrument	Grantor/Grantee or Testator
19 Oct [4 Chas I] 1628	101	Deed	Gyles Jones to Just Cooper et Ux
29 Sept 1629	103	Deed	Cooper et Ux to Fawdon & Weblin
25 Feb 1630	105	Assignmt	Weblin & Fawdon to Robt Sabin
21 Dec 1634	106	Assignmt	Robt Sabin to Chr Reynolds
[--] Dec 1634	15	Lease	Lacey to Gyar & Tooke
18 July 1636	11	Deed	Davis to Meador & White
13 Mar 1638	65	Grant	Jno Harvey to Peter Knight
25 Mar 1639	99	Deed	Anth Jones to Winchell & Smarley
1 May 1639	106	Deed	Chr Reynolds to Peter Hull
23 June 1640	20	Gift	Upton to Benn & ux
2 Apr [19 Chas I] 1643	2	Deed	Justinian Cooper to Alice Bennett
1 Dec 1643	87	Deed	Thomas Hinson to Wm Brunt
13 May 1644	28	Deed	John Pawley to Edward Wilmot
29 May 1644	52	Exchance	John Pawley to Richard Atkins
25 June 1644	98	Deed	Robt Eley to Wm Troloder
20 Aug 1644	28	Deed	Edward Wilmot to Henry White
12 Sept [20 Chas I] 1644	35	Grant	Richd Kemp to Robt Laurence
19 Oct 1644	87	Assignmt	Wm Brunt to Thomas Keerke
11 Jan 1645	99	Assignmt	Wm Troloder to Thomas Watton
25 Apr [21 Chas I] 1645	94	Deed	Just Cooper et Ux to Jno George
12 June 1645	53	Assignmt	Richard Atkins to Thomas Webb
23 Nov 1645	88	Assignmt	Thos Keerke to Nicholas Aldred
14 Mar 1646	107	Deed	Wm Yarrett to Thos Brandwood
15 Apr 1646	97	Deed	Edw Prince to Stephens et al
18 Apr 1646	100	Deed	Farrar Flinton to Jno Snellock
26 Oct 1646	17	Lease	James Tooke to Robert Harris

18 Jan 1647	14	Deed	Hobbs to Payne & Weeks
15 Feb 1647	19	Will	Edward Wilmouth
3 Mar 1647	17	Will	Richard Death
10 June 1647	4	Deed	James Roche to Henry Pitt
19 July 1647	4	Deed	Alice Bennett to Jackson daughters
27 Aug 1647	29	Deed	Henry White to George Stephens
21 Sept [23 Chas I] 1647	8	Deed	John Upton to Thos Greenwood
22 Sept [23 Chas I] 1647	5	Deed	John Upton to John Oliver
19 Oct 1647	12	Will	Roger Bagnall
29 Mar 1648	13	Deed	Robert Partin to John Seward
9 June [24 Chas I] 1648	10	Deed	John Upton to William Dawson
23 Sept 1648	23	Deed	Thomas Davis to John Moon
25 June [25 Chas I] 1649	21	Deed	Bennett to Motley & Turner
16 Aug 1649	25	Will	Anthony Jones
7 Sept 1649	113	Will	Edward Chetwine
9 Jan 1650	34	Deed	Jno Upton to John Valentine
14 Jan 1650	30	Will	John Vasser
2 Apr [26 Chas I] 1650	109	Deed	Amb Bennett to Ralph Warrener
7 Apr [26 Chas I] 1650	111	Deed	Amb Bennett to Amb Meador
26 Mar 1650	114	Will	Justinian Cooper
26 Dec 1650	29	Deed	Geo Stephens to Thomas Boswell
1 Jan 1651	26	Will	William Jewry
31 Jan 1651	1	Will	Timothy Fenn
6 Nov 1651	29	Will	Robert Watson
18 Nov 1651	32	Deed	Jno Upton to Wm Underwood
5 Dec 1651	90	Deed	Chr Lewis to John Gutteridge
[16 Jan 1652]	38	Will	John Upton
3 Feb 1652	40	Deed	Margaret Upton to Butcher
9 Apr 1652	41	Deed	Margaret Upton to Dewell
19 Apr 1652	79	Will	John Oliver
8 May 1652	30	Will	John Valentine
24 June 1652	33	Deed	Turner to Motly & Bennett
8 July 1652	36	Assignmt	Robt Laurence to Dnl Washborn
31 July 1652	42	Deed	John Sweet to Fra England
30 Sept 1652	45	Deed	Chr Lewis to John Burgess
26 Oct 1652	37	Will	John Stiles

1 Mar 1653	44	Will	Joseph Cobbs
21 Dec 1653	93	Deed	Geo Lobb/Atty to Rich Jordan
10 Apr 1654	90	Gift	Chas Barcroft to children
13 Mar 1654	68	Deed	Saml Eldridge to Hum Clark
1 May 1654	46	Will	Christopher Reynolds
27 Oct 1654	88	Gift	George Fawdon to Isaac George
30 Oct 1654	92	Marriage	Geo Fawdon & Ann Smith
16 Dec 1654	67	Deed	Sylv Thatcher to Anth Fulgham
29 Dec 1654	72	Deed	Henry Watts to John Sympson
31 Jan 1655	66	Grant	Peter Knight to James Innes
3 Mar 1655	70	Will	Humphrey Clark
8 Mar 1655	62	Deed	Margt Upton to Fra Slaughter
10 Mar 1655	69	Deed	James Watson to Henry Pitt
[10 May 1655]	75	Agreement	John Askue & John Hawkins
12 May 1655	76	P/o/A	Jno Nicholas to Wm Denbigh
14 May 1655	50	Assignmt	Lawrence Ward to Eliz King
9 July 1655	89	Confirmation	Nathll Bacon to Isaac George
[12 Aug 1655]	81	Will	John Moon
[10 Sept 1655]	88	Assignmt	Nicholas Aldred to Philip Parry
4 Feb 1656	57	Deed	Jervase Dodson to Harris
5 Feb 1656	58	P/o/A	Dodson to Fra Hobbs
28 Feb 1656	61	Deed	Taberer/Atty to Fra Ayers
7 Mar 1656	53	Deed	Cobbs to Samuel Haswell
[17 May 1656]	74	Will	Robert Dunster
9 Aug 1656	65	P/o/A	Margt Upton to John English
19 Nov 1656	59	P/o/A	Wm Thatcher to Fra Hobbs
24 Nov 1656	48	Will	Joshua Taberer
9 Dec 1656	51	Assignmt	George Lobb to John Brewer
4 July 1657	55	Deed	Yarrett to Bird et Ux
4 July 1657	56	Deed	Robert Bird et Ux Wm Yarrett
10 May 1658	79	Assignmt	Henry Moore
28 July 1658	77	Jury Decision	Snellock vs Hill
5 Feb 1659	115	Deed	Richd Young to Robert Pitt
2 Aug 1659	85	Deed	Druett et Ux to Thomas Elmes

As a final word on the importance of these documents, my feeling is that they must have been preserved because of their relevance to persons in the next century. Unfortunately, there are persons listed in the text who bear no *obvious* relation to eighteenth century Isle of Wight residents. Perhaps records will eventually surface which will reveal relationships between Isle of Wight's earliest inhabitants and its later colonials. For instance, later records demonstrate that one of testator Richard Death's Dodman descendants resided eventually in the Westmoreland Co., VA, area. His later descendants have not been traced, but it is hoped that these records will help elucidate links between the various counties.

I give thanks to Mr. Whitney Smith of Indianapolis, IN, and to Mrs. Anna WatSon for their expert help in proofreading.

John Anderson Brayton
Memphis, Tennessee
January 2001

ISLE OF WIGHT CO., VA, BOOK A

Isle of Wight County / Records: / containing a Transcript of divers Wills / Deeds Conveyances and other Antient Writings / collected from the primary Old Records which / lay Unbound in the Clerks Office. / Transcribed in the Year 1733

[original index] [1]

---

[1] In the original volume housed at the courthouse, a clerk has added entries to the index corresponding to missing letters "N-P."

MOON JOHN Will   81

      R [sic]
ROCHE JAMES to HENRY PITT Assignm^t 4
REYNOLDS CHRISTOPHER Will   46
REYNOLDS CH^r: to PETER HULL assigm^t: 106

      S
STILES JOHN Will   37
SWEET JN^O to FFRA^S: ENGLAND Deed   42
SABINE ROB^t: to REYNOLDS assig: 106

      T
TURNER to MOTLEY Deed   33
TABERNER JOSHUA Will   48
THATCHER to FFULGHAM Assignm^t 67
TROLODER to WOOTON assigm^t: 99

      V
UPTON JN^O to JN^O OLIVER Deed   5
UPTON JN^O to THO^S GREENWOOD Deed   8
UPTON JN^O to W^M: DAWSON Deed   10
Idem to XTOPHER BEN Cooper
      Deed of Gift   20
VASSER JOHN Will   30
VALENTINE JOHN Will   Idem
UPTON to UNDERWOOD Deed   32
UPTON to VALENTINE Deed   34
UPTON JOHN Will   38
UPTON MARGARETT Deed to BUTCHER   40
UPTON to DEWELL Deed   41
UPTON to SLAUGHTER Deed   62

      W
WILMOTH EDWARD Will   19
WATSON ROB^T nuncupitive will   29
WARD to KING Conveyance   50
WATSON to PITT Deed   69
WATTS HEN: to JN^O SYMPON [sic] Deed   72
WEBLING & FAWDON to SABINE assig: 105

[1]

In the Name of God Amen. / I TIMOTHY FENN being weak in Body but perfect in Sense / & Memory do make this my last Will & Testament. Imprimis / I bequeath my Soul to God my Saviour Jesus Christ and my / Body to the Earth to be buried in Christian Burial. Item / I Give & Bequeath unto my oldest Son Two Hundred Acres / of Land whereon I now live and One Hundred Acres of / the same Land I give & bequeath unto my youngest Son / my Wife having the Use of all the s^d three hundred Acres / of Land untill my Sons come to perfect Age and if in case / my eldest Son should die before he come to Age that then my Will / is that One hundred Acres of the said Land so given shall / return unto my Wife and the other Hundred unto my / Daughter. And as for my Land at Rappahannock if I / enjoy it I Give it to my three Children equaly to be / divided between them. Item I give & Bequeath unto / my Wife four Cows and all my Male Cattle only one Stear / for my ffuneral. Item I give & bequeath all my / young ffemale unto my three Children equaly to be divided / amongst them Item I Give unto my Daughter one ffeather Bed, and as for all the rest of my Goods & chattels / I give unto my Wife making her my whole Execu^rx desiring / my loving ffriends DANIEL BOUCHER & JOHN MUNGER / to be my Overseors of this my Will & Testament Witness / my hand this last of January 1651

Signed & delivered in   TIMOTHY **O** FENN
the Presence of   mark
GEORGE **x** GELLIE THO^S **x** DICKSON
        mark

Exam^d & truly Transcribed / Test JA^S: BAKER Cl Cur

[2]

This Indenture made the second / day of April in the Nineteenth Year of the Reign of our / Sovereign Lord King Charles of England Scotland ffrance & / &c Defender of the ffaith &c Between JUSTINNIAN COOPER of / the Isle of Wight County in Virginia Gent of the one party and / ALICE BENNETT Widdow on the other party Witnesseth / that the said JUSTINNIAN COOPER for and in Consideration of / one Cow one Calf and one Barrel of Corn to him in hand paid / by the said ALICE BENNETT before the ensealing & delivery / of these Presents Hath Given Granted Bargained Sold / Aliened Assigned and set over and doth by theses p^rsents / Give Grant Bargain Sell Alien Assign and set over unto / the said ALICE BENNETT her Heirs & Assigns for ever One /

Hundred & fifty Acres of Land Scituate lying & being in the / County of the Isle of Wight afores^d: lying between Castle Creek / and a Gut with a cypress Swamp Surveys East upon the old marked Tree / West into the Woods North towards Stockers South upon the / Lease Land to have and to Hold the s^d Land /bounded as af^d with her due shares of all Mines & Minerals / therein contained and with all Rights & Priviledges thereunto / belonging unto the s^d: ALICE BENNETT her Heirs, & Assigns for /ever in as large & ample manner & form to all Intents & / Purposes as the s^d: P^rmisses are or have been formerly / Granted to him ye s^d: JUSTINNIAN COOPER & his Heirs by vertue / of One Deed of Grant made by Sr WILLIAM BERKELLY Kn^t. Governor / and Captain General of Virginia under the Colony Seal of the / Province af^d and bearing Date the 16 of March 1642 / and in ye Eighteenth Year of his s^d Majesties Reign To / Have and to Hold the said forerecited p^rmisses / and every part & parcel thereof under the Tenures Rents / Services and Conditions in the said Deed of Grant mentioned and / expressed unto the said ALICE BENNETT her Heirs & Assigns / for ever And the said JUSTINNIAN COOPER for himself his

[3]

Heirs Executors Administrators & Assigns doth Covenant & grant / to and with the said ALICE BENNETT her Executors Adm^rs & Assigns that / he is at this present seized of an indefeazable Estate of ye p^rmisses / in fee Simple according to the Tenure & Purport of ye aforementioned / Deed of Grant and that the s^d p^rmisses are free & clear and / always made free & clear by the said JUSTINNIAN COOPER his Heirs / Executors Adm^rs & Assigns from all former Bargains Sales / Jointures Dowers Judgments Executions or any other Incumberances whatsoever had made done or suffered by the said JUSTINNIAN / COOPER And the said JUSTINNIAN COOPER doth by these / p^sents further Covenant & Grant to and with the said / ALICE BENNETT her Heirs & Assigns that he the said / JUSTINNIAN COOPER his Heirs Exec^rs & Adm^rs shall & will at / all times hereafter Warrant & Defend the s^d forerecited / p^rmisses to the said ALICE BENNETT her Heirs & Assigns / against him the said JUSTINNIAN COOPER his Heirs & Assigns / and against any other person or Persons whatsoever / Claiming by from or under him the s^d JUSTINNIAN COOPER / In Witness whereof the said Partie to these P^rsents hath set to him Hand & Seal the Day and Year / above written

JUSTINNIAN: COOPER

Signed Sealed & Delivered
In Presence of Us
JAMES TAYLOR SAMUEL ABBOTT

Exam^d & truly Transcribed / Teste JA^S: BAKER ClCur / Vide Assignment of the Land over Leaf

[4]

      This Witnesseth that I ALICE BENNETT / doth absolutely freely & voluntarily Give Pass over & Bequeath / all my Right & Title to this One Hundred & fifty Acres of / Land here within mentioned unto MARY & SARAH the / daughters of RICHARD JACKSON their Heirs Ex^{rs} Adm^{rs} / and Assigns (viz) all the Land and housing on this side / the Swamp where I now dwell I give unto MARY the Daughter / of RICHARD JACKSON and all ye Land on the other side the / Swamp unto SARAH the Daughter of RICHARD JACKSON wth / all the priviledges thereunto belonging Provided / that if either of these shall dye not having any Child / that then her Land shall wholly remain to the /Surviving party any thing Deed or Will hereafter made by me ALICE BENNETT in any wise notwithstanding / and that the Parties above mentioned shall be / possessed of the same Land immediately after my Decease / In Witness whereof I have hereunto set my / Hand & Seal 19th of July 1647
Test EDW^D x GARRETT JAMES PYLAND

                                  ALICE **B** BENNETT (Seal)

      Exam^d & truly Transcribed / Test JA^S: BAKER Cl. Cur

      Know all Man that I JAMES ROCHE of the County / of Isle of Wight by Vertue of an Assignment of a certain / parcel of Land & Housing lying in Chuckatuck Sold and made over unto me the said ROCHE by THOMAS / BRICE of the s^d Chuckatuck as by the s^d Assignment / bearing Date the 14th day of June 1643 at large / appeareth. Now know Y^e that I the s^d JAMES / have likewise Sold Assigned & made over and by these / ~~psents~~ do Sell Assign & make over unto Mr. HENRY / PITT all the said Parcel of Land Housing & App^{r}etences

[5]

with all Rights & Privelidges thereunto belonging excepting / only as in the s^d Assignment from THOMAS BRICE is / excepted To Have and to Hold the said / tract of Land Housing & Appurtenances with all Rights / and Priviledges afores^d unto the said HENRY PITT / his Heirs or Assigns for ever in as large and / ample manner as I the said JAMES ROCHE have / ever had unto the same In Witness whereof / I have hereunto set my Hand & Seal the 10th day of / June 1647
                              JAMES ROCHE (Seal)

Signed & Delivered
in the Presence of
GEORGE FOWDEN ANTHONY JONES

Accognitur in Curia nono Die Augsti 1647 / Teste THOMAS WOMBWELL Cl Cur / Examined & truly Transcribed / Teste JA^s: BAKER Cl Cur

This Indenture made the 22^d day of Sep^r / in the Twenty third Year of the Reign of our Sovreign / Lord Charles King of England Scotland ffrance and / Ireland Defender of the ffaith & Between Captain / JOHN UPTON Gen^t. Of the County of y^e Isle of Wight of / the one party and JOHN OLIVER Planter of the said / County Planter on the other party Witnesseth that / the said Capt JOHN UPTON for a full & valuable Consider= / =ation unto him by the s^d JOHN OLIVER well & truly / contented & paid at and before the ensealing hereof / whereof and wherewith the said Captain JOHN UPTON

[6]
Acknowledgeth himself well & truly Contented & Paid / and thereof and of every part thereof doth as well for / himself as also his Heirs Executors & Administrators / clearly acquit and discharge the said JOHN OLIVER / his Heirs Executors & Adm^{rs} by these p^{r}sents hath / Bargained Sold Granted Assigned & Sett over and / by these P^{r}sents doth fully clearly & absolutely / Bargain Sell Grant Assign & set over unto the / said JOHN OLIVER his Heirs Executors Adm^{rs} & Assignes / for ever One hundred Acres of Land scituate lying / and being in the County aboves^d being part of a / of four Hundred Acres due unto him the / said Captain JOHN UPTON by patent Beginning / at a Tree marked with a V and extending from / thence a Mile into the Woods running upon the / westerly Line of the s^d Dividend abutting & adjoining / upon ye Land of Mr JUSTINIAN COOPER, Northerly / upon James River Easterly upon the Land of / THOMAS GREENWOOD and Southerly into the Main Wood / which said Land was lately in the Possession and / Occupation of JOHN SMITH To have & hold / and Peaceable enjoy the said Land with / all Houses Ediffices Orchards Gardens Medows and / Marshes with all Priviledges ffreedoms Immolum^{ts} / and Immunities thereunto belonging thereon being / or therein included ffurthermore the said / Capt. JOHN UPTON doth hereby Bargain & Sell as / afs^d all Deeds Charters Evidences writings / and Escripts which he or any other Person or / Persons to his Use had or have concerning the / P^{r}misses or any Parcel thereof the said Captain

[7]
JOHN UPTON Hereby affirming and Warranting this to / be a lawful Deed of Sale discharging and acquitting / the said JOHN OLIVER &c from all former Bargains / Annuities Fees Jointures Extents Lease final or Condemnations / and

of all Incumberance whatsoever except The Rents and / Service due to the Kings most Excellent majesty from / henceforth to be paid all Arrearages of Rent or former / Service to be paid by the s^d Captain JOHN UPTON Lastly / The s^d Captain JOHN UPTON covenanteth that he and all other / persons at any time seized to his use in the P^{r}mises / Shall at all times before the first Day of April next / coming suffer and cause to be done & Suffered all and / every such Thing & Things as shall tend or conduce / to the further Confirmation & Establishment of this Sale / unto the said JOHN OLIVER his Heirs Executors Adm^{rs} / assigns for Ever with further Warranty against all / Counter Claims or Oppositions whatsoever Peaceably to / Have Hold & Enjoy the premises with all Appurtenances / without any Lett Eviction or Expulsion of the said / Captain JOHN UPTON his Heirs &c or any other Persons / by reason of any other Claim or Title had or grown / before the Date hereof In Witness of which / Bargain Sale Covenant Grant on ye Behalf of the / s^d Captain JN^O UPTON to be performed and truly done / he hath hereunto set his Hand & Seal the Day and / Year above-mentioned
Sealed Signed and   JOHN UPTON (Seal)
Deliv^d in p^{r}sence of Us
PETER KNIGHT JAMES PYLAND

Examin^d & truly Transcribed / Teste JA^S: BAKER ClCur

[8]
      This Indenture made the Twenty / first day of September in the Twenty third Year of the Reign / of our Sovereign Lord Charles King of England Scotland / & ffrance & Between Captain JOHN UPTON Gent of the County / of the Isle of Wight of the one party and THOMAS GREENWOOD / planter of the same County Witnesseth that the s^d Captain / JOHN UPTON for a full & valuable Consideration unto him / by the said THOMAS GREENWOOD well & truly contented and / paid at and before the ensealing hereof whereof and / wherewith the said Captain JOHN UPTON acknowledgeth / himself well & truly contented & paid and thereof and / every part thereof doth as well for himself as his Heirs / Executors & Adm^{rs} clearly Acquit & Discharge the said THOMAS / GREENWOOD his Heirs Ex^{rs} & Adm^{rs} by those P^{r}sents / Hath Bargained Sole Assigned & Set over and by / these P^{r}sents doth fully clearly & absolutely Bargain Sell / Grant Assign and set over unto the said THOMAS GREENWOOD his / Heirs Executors Adm^{rs} & Assigns for ever One Hundred Acres of / Land lying & being in the County aboves^d being part of a / Dividend of four Hundred Acres due unto him the said / Captain JOHN UPTON by Patent the said One Hundred Acres being / bounded Northerly upon James River Westerly upon one / hundred Acres of Land sold by the s^d Captain JNO UPTON / to JOHN OLIVER being part of the said Dividend running / Southerly unto ye Woods and adjoining

Easterly upon the / other two hundred Acres the residue of the said Dividend / To have Hold & peaceable to enjoy / the said one Hundred Acres of Land with all Houses Ediffices / Gardens Orchards Woods Meadows Marshes with all / priviledges freedoms Immunities & Emoluments / thereunto belonging thereon being or therein included / Furthermore the said Captain JOHN UPTON doth

[9]

hereby Bargain & Sell as aforesaid all Deeds Charters / Evidences Writings which he or any other person or Persons / to his Use had or have concerning the P^{r}misses or any / parcel thereof the sd Captain UPTON hereby affirming and / Warranting this to be a lawful Deed of Sale discharging / and Acquitting the sd THOMAS GREENWOOD his Heirs Ex^{rs} / Adm^{rs} & Assigns from all former Bargains Annuities / ffees ffines Jointures Extents Leases or Condemnations / and of all Incumberances whatsoever except ye Services / & Rents due to the Kings most excellent Majesty from / henceforth to be paid all Arrearages of Services or / former Rents to be paid by the said Captain JOHN UPTON / Lastly the said Captain JOHN UPTON covenanteth that / he and all other persons of any time Seized to his Use in / the p^{r}misses shall at all times before the first of April / next coming suffer and cause to be done & suffered all / and every such Thing & Things as shall tend or conduce / to the further Confirmation & Establishment of this Sale / unto the said THOMAS GREENWOOD his Exe^{rs} Admin^{rs} or / Assigns for ever with further Warranty against all counter / Claims or Oppositions whatsoever Peaceably to Enjoy / Have & Hold the p^{r}misses without any Lett Expulsion / Eviction of the said Captain UPTON his Heirs or any other / persons by reason of any other Claim or Title had or / grown before The Date hereof. In Witness of which / said Bargain Sale Covenant & Grant on the Behalf of the said Captain UPTON to be truly performed he hath hereunto set / his Hand & Seal the Day and Year above mentioned
Signed Sealed & Delivered
in Presence of Us   JOHN UPTON (Seal)
PETER KNIGHT JAMES PYLAND

Exam^d and truly Transcribed / Teste JA^S: BAKER ClCur

[10]

This Indenture made the Ninth day of / June in the Twenty fourth Year of the Reign of our / Sovereign Lord Charles King of England &c Between / Captain JOHN UPTON Gent on the one party and WILLIAM / DAWSON Planter on the other Party both of the County of the Isle of / Wight Witnesseth that y^e said Captain JOHN UPTON for a / full and valuable Consideration to him by the said DAWSON well / and truly contented & paid at and before the ensealing / hereof whereof and wherewith the said Captain UPTON acknow= / =ledgeth & paid and thereof and / of every part thereof doth clearly Acquit & discharge the s^d. / WILLIAM DAWSON his Heirs Executors & Administrators for / ever Hath Bargained & Sold and by these P^rsents / clearly Bargaineth & Selleth to the said WILLIAM DAWSON his / Heirs &c for ever One / Hundred Acres of Land scituate / and being in the County af^d bounded with a Creek called / Hutchensons Creek on the East part thereof on the South / with a tract of Land called the Indian ffeild with the / woods on the West on the North with the Land now in / the Occupation of WILLIAM CLAPHAM To Have Hold / and Peaceably to enjoy the same with all Houses Orchards / Gardens Meadows & Marshes thereon being or therein / included with all priviledges ffredoms Imoluments or / Immunities thereof being or thereunto belonging unto the / said DAWSON as af^d and his Heirs for ever Also the said / Captain UPTON doth hereby acknowledge this Deed of Sale / to be good against all Persons with Warranty dischar= / =ging and acquitting the said DAWSON from all former / Bagains Sales ffees Jointures Dowers Leases Fines / Judgments and Executions and of all other Incumberances / or Charges whatsoever except the Rent & Services due to / the Kings most excellent Majesty from henceforth to be / paid the said Captain UPTON Covenanting furthermore

[11]

to discharge the said DAWSON of and from all Arrears of Rent / grown or being due before these presents Moreover the / said Captain UPTON Covenanteth & Granteth unto all and / every Person or Persons unto whom the said DAWSON may / or shall Bargain & Sell the said One Hundred Acres of / Land with the Appurtenances or any part or parcel / thereof to them and their Heirs peaceable to Have / Hold & Enjoy the same without any Lett Expulsion / Eviction of the said Captain UPTON his Heirs &c. or any / other Person by reason of any Title had or grown before / the Date hereof. In Witness of which Sale, Bargain / Covenant & Grant on the Behalf of the said Captain / JOHN UPTON to be truly performed and done he hath / hereunto put his Hand & Seal the Day and Year / above mentioned

Signed Sealed &   JOHN UPTON (Seal)
Deliv^d in Prsence of Us
JAMES WILLIAMSON THO^S WOMBWELL

Exam^d & truly Transcribed / Teste JA^S: BAKER ClCur

Know ye by these presents that I THOMAS / DAVIS of Warwicksqueak have Sold unto AMBROSE / MEADOR & JOHN WHITE of the Pagan Shoare their / Heirs Exec^{rs}: Adm^{rs}: or Assigns the quantity of Fifty Acres / of Land for ever lying in Warwicksqueak beginning / at the Upper red Point extending Easterly down

[12]

the said Creek with all the Rights & Priviledges / thereunto belonging in as large and ample manner / as was given unto the said Thomas by his patent / and Granted unto him by the Governour & Council / the Sixth day of March Anno 1633 the afores^d. Land / abutting Northerly upon the s^d. Creek and Southerly / into the Main Wood In Witness whereof / I have hereunto set my Hand & Seal this present / 18th day of July 1636

Sealed Signed & Delivered   THO^S: DAVIS (Seal)

in presence of

THOMAS HOLT   RICHARD LEE

       Exam^d & truly Transcribed / Teste JA^S: BAKER ClCur

       In the Name of God Amen. / The last Will & Testam^t of ROGER BAGNALL being very Sick / of Body but in his perfect Sense & Memory thanks / be to God. I Bequeath my Body to the Ground / and my Soul unto God that gave it. I Give / and Bequeath unto my Wife REBECCA BAGNELL two / Cows and two Heifers of two Year old a piece, and two / Yearling Heifers, and that the afores^d REBECCA do make / good for the Use of the Children if the Estate will hold / out One Yearling Heifer a piece Unto each of my / Children one to be delivered, or to run for their Use / from the first day of April which shall be in ye Year / 1649 I do further Bequeath unto my Wife REBECCA / BAGNALL all my Goods Household stuff and whatsoever / doth belong unto the said ROGER BAGNALL as Crops of

[13]

Corn or Tobacco or Hoggs, Land and Plantation likewise; until / my Son JAMES BAGNALL shall be a lawful Heir himself / And likewise whatever Debts, Bills, or Accounts that is / by Bill or Account due unto me I here give & bequeath / them unto my Wife. Item. I Give & Bequeath unto / my Son JAMES BAGNALL when he is of Age to enjoy it / the Plantation I now live on unto the said JAMES / and his Heirs for ever, with all the Housing and / Priviledge thereunto belonging. And unto this / this my last Will & Testament I have hereunto set / my Hand this 19th of October 1647

Signed in Presence of   ROGER **B** BAGNALL

JOSEPH: WEEKS   CHA^S: STEWART

       Exam^d and truly Transcribed / Teste JA^S: BAKER ClCur

Be it known unto all Men / by these presents that I ROBERT PARTIN of the Isle of Wight / have made Sole & set over And I do firmly by these / Presents Deliver make Sell & set over unto JN^O SEWARD / of the afores^d County one Plantation whereon I now live / and likewise two draw & Oxen being Black cropt and / slit in both Ears between Six & Seven Year of Age / Also one Stear being Brown being cropt & slit in both / Ears. Likewise two Cows being red marked as afores^d / Also I the above named ROBERT PARTIN do bind me / my Heirs Executors Adm^{rs} & Assigns that the sd JOHN SEWARD / His Heirs Executors Adm^{rs} & Assigns shall Enjoy the / aboves^d Cattle with their Increase, likewise ye plantation / Peaceable and quit without any Trouble or Molestation

[14]
of me my Heirs & Assigns or any other manner of / Person or Persons whatsoever And if any Person or / Persons shall lay any Claim Right or Title to the said / Plantation or Chattels that I the said ROBERT PARTIN now / bind me my Heirs & Assigns to save & keep harmless / the said STEWARD upon ye payment of Two Thousand / Eight Hundred and Thirty Pounds of Tobacco with / Cask bearing date the same day specified by / Specialty the abovenamed Chattels and Plantation / to be Redelivered up to the said ROBERT PARTIN / which Tobacco is to be paid upon the 10th Day / of October next As Witness my Hand this / 29th March 1648
Signed and Deliv^d ROBERT PARTTIN
in the Psence of Us
JOHN ELLINGER FFRA^S E LAMBERT

       Exam^d & truly Transcribed / Test JA^S: BAKER ClCur

       Know all Men by these Presents that / I FFRANCIS HOBBS hath Sold Bargained & made Sale unto / JOHN PAYNE & JOSEPH WEEKS a Plantation that he enjoyed / by Lease bounded & scituated upon Nancimond River and / according to that full Power Right & Title that any shall / or can enjoy by Virtue of that Lease I the afores^d / HOBBS doth Assigns Convey make over and Confirm / Insure and make Good The Sale thereof from me / my Heirs Exec^{rs} Adm^{rs} or Assigns unto ye af^d PAYNE & WEEKS / jointly their Heirs Exec^{rs} Adm^{rs} or Assigns for ever / And do bind my self to Defend & Maintain

[15]
this Sale & Lease from any Person or Persons w^{t}soever / that shall disquiet or any wise disturb their quiet / Enjoyment & possession of the Land afores^d Unto / which Assignment & have hereunto set my Hand / This 18th Day of January 1647
Signed & Delivered   FRANCIS F HOBBS

in the Presence of Us
JOHN ELLINGER FFRAN^S E LAMBERT

Exam^d & truly Transcribed / Teste JA^S: BAKER ClCur

This Indenture made the [--] / of December Anno Dom 1634 and in the Tenth Year of y^e/ Reign of our Sovereign Lord King Charles by the Grace / of God of England Scotland ffrance and Ireland & Virginia / Defender of the ffaith &c Between WILLIAM LACEY / of Yarmouth in the Isle of Wight[2] Marriner Assignee / for ye heires of Captain ROBERT GYAR of the one party / and JAMES TOOKE of Warwicksqueak planter of y^e / other party Witnesseth that the s^d WILLIAM LACEY / for divers good Causes & Considerations him hereunto / specialy moving Hath Demised Leased Granted / and to Farm lett and by these p^{r}sents doth demise / Lease Grant & unto ffarm lett unto the s^d JAMES TOOKE / his Heirs Exec^{rs} Adm^{rs} or Assigns five Hundred Acres of Land scituate lying & being in Warwicksqueak / afors^d on the Easterly side of the Mouth of Lawnes / Creek being a Neck of land bounding & Cutting East / and by North and North and by West To have / and to Hold all and singular the s^d Land

[16]
and p^{r}mises unto the said JAMES TOOKE his Heirs and / Assigns during the Term of One & Twenty Years to / begin at the Birth of our Lord God next ensuing the / Date hereof Yeilding & Paying during the s^d Term / unto the s^d WILLIAM LACEY yearly or his Assigns or four / Hundred pounds of good Tobacco if it be lawfully / demanded And the said WILLIAM LACEY for himself / his Heirs Executors Adm^{rs} & Assigns doth Covenant / Promise & Grant to and with & with the s^d JAMES TOOKE / his Exec^{ors} & Assigns that the said JAMES TOOKE / his Heirs Exec^{rs} Adm^{rs} & Assigns shall and will / Peaceably & Quietly have hold occupy possess / and Enjoy all & singular ye p^{r}mises and Land / during the s^d Term of Twenty one Years wthout / the Lett Trouble molestation or Eviction of him / the s^d WILLIAM LACEY or his Assigns or any other / person or persons whatsoever In Witness / whereof the said Parties have interchangably set their Hands & Seals the Day and Year above / written
WILLIAM LACEY
Sealed and Delivered
in the presence of us
JOHN BUTLER JOHN SMITH

I do Confirm and Allow this Lease allways / provided he extend no further into the / Neck than the Easterly side of the plantation / of Mr LAWSON

---

[2] This is the one in England, under the jurisdiction of Hampshire.

he paying the former rent / Witness my Hand the 25th of July 1642 / THO[s] GYAR / Vide Assigmn[t] P̶ Contra

[17]

     I JAMES TOOKE Assign all my Right & Title of / this Lease unto ROBERT HARRIS this 26 of October / 1646 whereunto I have set my Hand Witness present   JAMES TOOKE
ROBERT WOODROSE THO[S] GYAR

     These Assignm[ts] now endorsed on the Lease / Test THO WOMBULL / Examined and truly Transcribed / Teste JA[S]: BAKER C[l] C[ur]

     In the Name of God. Amen. / I RICHARD DEATH of the Isle of Wight County in / Virginia being very sick & weak of Body but of / perfect Mind & Memory praised be God do hereby / make & ordain this my last Will & Testament / in manner and form Following First I commit / my Soul into the Hands of Almighty God my Creator / hoping & assuredly believing through the Mercies & / Merits of Jesus Christ my Saviour to receive free / pardon & remission of all my Sins, and my Body / to the Earth to be buried at the Discretion of my / Executors hereafter named but as concerning all / such Worldly Estate wherewith it hath pleased / God to endow me (my Debts which of Right / or Conscience I owe unto any Man being first paid & / satisfied) I give & bequeath (viz) Imprimis / I give and bequeath unto the Child my daughter / ELIZBETH DODMAN Wife of JOHN DODMAN now / goeth withal one Cow Calf already calved by the / Cow called Wests old Cow, but if it shall happen

[18]

the said Child dye before it comes to Age then the said Cow / Calf with her Increase I give unto JOHN DODMAN son of / the said JOHN DODMAN Item I Give & Bequeath unto / the said JOHN DODMAN jun[r] & RICHARD DODMAN son / of the sd JOHN DODMAN Sen[r] one Moyety or half of / such Goods Chattels Lands Movables & Immovables as / shall be the Estate of me the said RICHARD DEATH my / debts being first satisfied as af[d]. But if it shall / happen the said JOHN or RICHARD should dye or depart / this Life before they attain the Age of One and / Twenty Years that then he that shall be surviving to / possess the Estate of the other so deceased And if it / shall happen that both the said JOHN & RICHARD / depart this life before the sd Age of One and Twenty Years / that then the Estate bequeathed to belong & come unto / ELIZABETH the Wife of the said JOHN DODMAN. Item. / I Give & Bequeath unto WILLIAM DEATH my Son Citizen / and Merchant Taylor of London the other Moyety / or Half part of such Goods as shall be the Estate of / m the s[d]

RICHARD DEATH as af^d as Goods Chattels / Land Movables & Immovables but if it shall happen / WILLIAM DEATH shall be departed this Mortal / Life that then the Estate bequeathed unto him I Give / and Bequeath unto JOHN & RICHARD DODMAN as af^d. / Sons of the said JOHN DODMAN Item. I Give and / Bequeath unto CHRISTOPHER NEAL son of DANIEL NEAL / of the Isle of Wight County af^d one Cow Calf of any / of the Cattle of me the s^d RICHARD DEATH which shall / be next Calved. Item. I will that the Estate bequeathed / as aforesaid unto JOHN & RICHARD DODMAN Sons of the / s^d JOHN DODMAN remain in the Hands & Custody of / the s^d JOHN DODMAN Senr until they shall attain / unto the Age of One and Twenty Years. And of this

[19]

my last Will & Testament do make & ordain the said / JOHN DODMAN Senr my Sole & full Executor and do / Renounce all former Wills & Testaments. In Witness / whereof I the said RICHARD DEATH unto this my last / Will and Testament have set my Hand & Seal this / Third day of March 1647

Sealed & Delivered   RICH^D. DEATH (Seal)
In Presence of
WILLIAM WESTWRAY

Examined & truly Transcribed / Test JA^S: BAKER ClCur

In the name of God Amen. I EDWARD WILMOTH being at this time very weak in / Body but perfect of Memory praised be God for it / I bequeath my Body to the Earth from whence it was first / taken and also my Soul into the Hands of Goe my / faithful Creator who hath made all Mankind to whom / be Honour & Glory both now and for ever. Imprimis / I do by these Presents make my beloved Wife ANNIS WILMOTH / my full & whole Executrix of all my Goods & Chattels / God hath given unto me in Virginia or elsewhere / particularly I give unto my Wife af^d four Milch Cows / a Steer and an Heifer that is on Lawns Creek side / and a young Yearling Bull. Also I give unto my / Daughter FFRANCES a Yerling Heifer, and if this Heifer / should dye in the mean time my Wife shall make / it good out of her own Stock. Also I give unto my / Son JOHN WILMOTH a Cow Calf and to my Son ROBERT / WILMOTH a Cow Calf and if those Cow Calves should / miscarry my Wife ANNIS WILMOTH shall make them

[20]

good out of her own Stock. Also if any of these / Children dye before they come to Age it is my Will / the said Cattle shall come to the Survivour. Also / the plantation that we are Upon I give unto my / Wife and all my Household Stuff &

Movables / Also I entreat JOHN JACKSON & GEORGE COBOROFT / to be my Overseers for performance of my last / Will & Testament being a true Act & Deed of / mine own Witness my Hand this 15th Day / of ffebruary 1647
Test. JOHN JACKSON. JOHN CARTER   EDWARD WILMOTH

Examined & truly Transcribed / Test JA^S: BAKER ClCur

To all People to whom these Presents shall / Come to be Seen I Captain JOHN UPTON of the Isle / of Wight County of Virginia send Greeting Know Ye / that I the said Capt. JOHN UPTON for the Love & Natural / Affection I have and do bear unto CHRISTOPHER / BEEN Cooper and ANN his Wife Have Given Granted / and Confirmed and by these P^rsents do Give Grant & / Confirm unto the s^d CHRISTOPHER BENN his Heirs and / Assigns for Ever One piece or parcel of Land containing / fifty Acres be it more or less scituate lying & being at / the head of the Creek called Pagan Creek within the / County af^d extending in Length from the point there called / The Piney Point N:E unto other ye Land there of / the said Capt JOHN UPTON and in Breadth there from / the Point used for a Landing Place belonging unto

[21]
the Land in the Occupation of THOMAS JONES N:E unto / a Creek there called the Cross Creek S:E together with / all Profits & commodities & appertenances to the said / Land belonging or appertaining. To have and / to Hold the said ffifty Acres of Land hereby / Granted and every part thereof unto the said XTOFER / BENN his Heirs & Assigns to the only proper Use of / the said CHRISTOPHER BENN his Heirs & Assigns for ever / In Witness whereof I the said Captain JOHN / UPTON have hereunto set my Hand & Seal Dated / The 23^d day of June Anno 1640
Sealed & delivered   JOHN UPTON (Seal)
in Presence of me
RICHARD WILLIAMSON

Examined & truly Transcribed / Test JA^S: BAKER ClCur

This Indenture made the 25th day of / June in the Twenty fifth Year of our Sovereign Lord / Charles & Between AMBROSE BENNET of the one / party and JOHN MOTLEY & THOMAS TURNER of the / other party Planters Witnesseth that the said / AMBROSE BENNETT for a full & valuable Consideration / unto him by the sd MOTLEY & TURNER before the / ensealing hereof whereof & wherewith the said AMBROSE BENNETT hereby acknowledgeth himself / well & truly contented & paid and thereof and / every part thereof doth as well for himself as / his Heirs &c clearly Acquit & Discharge the said / MOTLEY & TURNER their Heirs &c by these Presents / Hath Bargained Assigned and Set over And / by these Psents Doth fully clearly & absolutely

[22]
Bargain Sell Assigne & Set over unto the said MOTELY & / TURNER their Heirs &c for ever Two Hundred Acres of / Land scituate & being in the County of Isle of Wight / being part of a Dividend of Eleven Hundred Acres of / Land due unto the said AMBROSE BENNETT by a Patent / Signed under the Hand of the late Governour S^r. / FFRANCIS WYATT on which Patent there is fifty Acres / added thereunto belonging unto HOPKIN HOWEL / which said Two Hundred Acres is bounded according / as in the S^d Patent is expressed bearing Date the / 23^d day of June Anno 1644 may appear and is / the utmost Westerly Bounds of the af^d Dividend / of Eleven Hundred Acres of Land lying between y^e / Land also of HENRY FFREESTONE Part of the said / Dividend and ye af^d ffifty Acres belonging unto / HOPKIN HOWEL proportionably bearing Length & / Breadth according to the S^d Patent To have / and to Hold and Peaceably to Enjoy the said / Two Hundred Acres with all Priviledges &t And / Moreover the said AMBROSE BENNETT doth hereby / sell &c all Deeds Evidences &c which concern / the premisses unto the said MOTELY &c freeing them &c / from all Incumberances Bargains & Extents &c / whatsoever Except the Rents & Service due to the / Kings most Excellent Majesty from henceforth due / to be paid with further Warranty against all Claims / Countermands or Opposition whatsoever Peaceably to / enjoy the P^{r}misses &c In Witness of which / Bargain & Sale Covenant & Grant on the behalf / of the said AMBROSE BENNETT to be truly / performed he hath hereunto put his Hand & Seal

[23]
the Day and Year above
signed Sealed & Deliv^d AMBROSE A BENNETT
in the P^{r}sence of Us   mark   (Seal)
ROB^T PRICE HOPKIN HOWEL GEORGE RAWLES

Further Conveyed vide fo: (79)

Exm^d & truly Transcribed / Test JA^S: BAKER ClCur

To all Christian People to whome these / presents shall come I THOMAS DAVIS of Nancemond / Gent send Greeting in our Lord God Everlasting / Whereas S^r. JOHN HARVEY K^t. Governour &c did with / the Consent of the Council of State by his Letters Patent / dated the sixth of March 1643 Give and

Grant unto / me the said THOMAS DAVIS Three Hundred Acres of / Land scituate & being within the Limmits of Warwick= / squeak and abutting on the Easterly side of y^e Creek / known by the Name of Warwicksqueak Creek about two / Miles from the Mouth of the s^d Creek bounding and / beginning Easterly at Point of Land called the / Red Point and thence extending Westerly by the s^d / Creek abutting Northerly upon the s^d Creek & & Southerly / into The Woods To have and to Hold / the said Three Hundred Acres of Land with the / Appurtenances as by the said Letters Patent will appear / Now Know Ye that I the said THOMAS DAVIS / for and in Consideration of Two Thousand Pounds / of Tobacco by me in Hand received wherewith I / Acknowledge my self fully satisfied & Contented as / also for divers other Considerations Have Aliened / Bargained Sold Assigned and make over And

[24]

by these Presents Alien &c unto JOHN MOON of the County / of Isle of Wight Gent Two Hundred Acres of Land / out of the afore mentioned Three hundred Acres To have / and to Hold the said Two hundred Acres with / all Rights Priviledges Commodities & Emoluments w^{t}soever / to the same belonging or any wise Appertaining to him / the said JOHN MOON his Heirs Executors Adm^{rs} & Assigns / for ever in as large & ample manner as I the / said THOMAS DAVIS might or could have had by / Vertue of the s^d Letters Patents And I the / said THOMAS DAVIS do for me my Heirs & further Promise / & Covenant to save defend & keep harmless the said / JOHN MOON his Heirs Executors &c from any Claim / Title or Interest of any Person or Persons w^{t}soever / claiming from by or under him with any Leases / already long since granted (only excepted until their / Expiration) And I the said THOMAS DAVIS / do further Covenant & Promise for me my Heirs &c / at all times within Seven Years to come at the / reasonable Request & Charges of the s^d JOHN MOON / &c to Give & Make or cause to be Made such other / further Assurance & Conveyance of the s^d Two hundred / Acres of Land as he or his Council in the Law / shall Advise In Witness of the Premisses I the / said THOMAS DAVIS have hereunto set my Hand & Seal the 23^d of September Anno 1648
Signed Sealed & Deliv^d THOMAS DAVIS (Seal)
in Presence of
THO^S HAWOOD PETER KNIGHT THOMAS WOMBWELL

Vide Edictum & Contra[3]

[25]

Accognitur in Curia Insula Vectis xj^o Die / Decembris Annoq^u 1648[4]

---

[3] "See the verdict and against."

Test me THO^S: WOMBWELL Cl ꝑ dicta Curia^5

Examined & truly Transcribed / Test JA^S: BAKER ClCur

In the name of God Amen / the 16th day of August 1649 I ANTHONY JONES of / the Isle of Wight County in Virginia being in weak / estate of Body but sound Memory & perfect do make / my last Will & Testament as followeth Imprimis / I bequeath my Soul to God my Creator and my body / to the Earth from whence it came / And of my Goods / which God hath given me Item I bequeath to my / Brother WILLIAM JONES if so be he comes to live in the / Country four Cows one Servant, one ffeather Bed, one / Stear and Corn sufficient for the Year with that / Plantation where THOMAS PARKER lived to be fitted up / for him But, and if he come in a Single Man to live / with my Wife in this my now dwelling House Plantation / or if in Case he have a Desire to return Home again / with the Shipping, to have Three Thousand Pounds of / Tobacco sent him Home the next Year and Two / Thousand this Year. Item I give to my Daughter / in Law ANN SMITH the Plantation I now live on / with the Dividend of Land thereunto belonging / after my Wife's decease Item I Give to my / Syster CATHERINE JONES Five Pounds Sterling / to be paid her at the return of the Ships if she / be living Item I bequeath to my Godson

[26]
ANTHONY BEUFORD one Heifer to be paid the Next May / Item I Give & Bequeath to THOMAS & JOHN SMITH / all my Land due to take up at the Black Water or / elsewhere which is Two Thousand Acres as is Recorded / at James Town and that it be divided into two / parts each to have a several Patent by himself / Item I make my Wife ANN my whole & sole / Executrix of all my Goods & Chattles whatsoever after / my Debts are paid
Signed Sealed and   ANTHONY JONES (Seal)
carefully Perused
ROBERT WATSON EDW^D. CHETWOOD THOMAS BRASEE

Exam^d and truly Recorded / Test JA^S: BAKER ClCur.

In the Name of God Amen. / I WILLIAM JEWRY of the Isle of Wight County being / very Sick & Weak but of perfect Mind & Memory / praised be God do hereby make my last Will & / Testament in manner & form following

---

⁴ "Acknowledged in Isle of Wight County Court the 11th day of December and in the year 1648."
⁵ "I, as witness, Thomas Wombwell, clerk of the aforesaid court."

(Viz) / First I commit my Soul into the Hands of Almighty / God my Maker & Creator hoping & assuredly believing / thro' ye Mercies & Merits of Jesus Xt. My Saviour and / Redeemer to receive free Pardon & Remission of all / my Sins and my Body to the Earth from whence it / came to be decently Buried at the Discretion of / my Executor hereafter named in Parish Church of / this County aboves^d. But as concerning all such / Worldly Estate wherewith it hath pleased God to / endue me I give & bequeath in fform Following

[27]
After my Debts which I Justly owe unto any Man being first / paid and my ffuneral Expences Satisfied Imprimis I Give / and Bequeath unto ELIZABETH PENNY the daughter of RICHARD PENNY / of the County afores^d One Yearling Cow Calf. Item I Give / and Bequeath unto ROBERT RUFFIN Son of WILLIAM RUFFIN of / The Isle of Wight County af^d one black Heifer with two / white ffeet behind of two Years old of the proper Mark / of me the s^d WILLIAM JEWRY. Item I Give & Bequeath / unto JOHN ARRAM Son of JOHN ARRAM of the County / af^d the Calf the my red Heifer now goeth withal / all & singular the rest of my Estate I Give & bequeath / unto my dear & Loving ffriend ye af^d JN^O ARRAM for / and of this my last Will & Testament do make & ordain / him full & Sole Executor In Witness whereof I / the said WILLIAM JEWRY Renouncing all former Wills / to this my last Will & Testament have set my Hand / the ffirst of January Anno Domini 1651
Signed and Delivered   WILLIAM **O** JEWRY
in the Presence of Us
RICHARD **R:P**: PENNY WILLIAM **WR** RUFFIN WILLIAM WESTWRAY

     This Will was proved in Court the ixth of April / ꝑ Sacrament of RICHARD PENNY & WILLIAM RUFFIN

     Examin^d & truly Transcribed / Test JA^S: BAKER ClCur

[28]
     This Indenture mad [sic] the 13th. of May 1644 Between / JOHN PAWLEY & EDWARD WILMOT Witnesseth that the said / JOHN PAWLEY for himself &t. have Aliened &t. unto the S^d. EDWARD / WILMOT &t. for Ever One Hundred Acres of Land which he the S^d. / PAWLEY took up for the Said WILMOT for Transportation of Two / Servants and also the Sd. PAWLEY for himself his Heirs Executors / Adm^{rs} & Assigns do Alien enfeoff & Confirm unto the S^d. WILMOT / his Heirs &t. all the overplus Land Adjoyining unto the WILMOTs / Hundred Acres be it more or less being one Entire Neck which / Overplus the Said JOHN PAWELEY fort the Consideration of Seven / Hundred pounds of Tobacco sold to him the Said WILMOT his Heirs / &t. in fee simple

for Ever Beginning upon the South East side / of the Mill pond, Southerly along a Swamp & East upon Capt: / BERNARD his Marked Trees being the South East Bounds of his / the s^d JOHN PAWLEYs Land which Land is Scituate in James City / County Bounded in Manner following, North upon THOMAS / STAMPE East upon Lawnes Creek, South along the Creek & West / into the Woods as by Pattent to PAWLEY of the 18th. of June / 1639. To Have and to Hold all the S^d. Hundred / Acres of Land with all the overplus in the S^d. Neck contained / from him the S^d. PAWLEY his Heirs &t. for Ever, with all / rights &t. in the S^d. Pattent contained Yealding & paying / unto his Majestie &t. two Shillings yearly after the S^d. EDWARD &t. / hath lived thereon 7 years as by the S^d. PAWLEYs Pattent may / Appear. And the S^d. JOHN PAWLEY for Himself his Heirs &t. / doth Covenant &t. to the S^d. EDWARD WILMOT his Heirs &t. that he / and they Shall peaceably &t. have hold &t. all & Singular the Said / Lands &t. without the Lawfull Let Trouble &t. of the S^d. PAWLEY / his Heir &t. In Witness the parties aboves^d. Have Interchang= / =ably Set their hands & Seals the day & year above Said

Signed Sealed & delivered   JOHN PAWLEY
in Presence of
JOHN GEORGE JAMES DRAKE

      Be it Known unto all men that I EDWARD WILMOT / have Sold and turned over all my right & Title herein / Specified unto HENRY WHITE his Heirs & Assigns for Ever / Wi^{t}ness my hand this 20th. of August 1644
Test DANIELL BOUCHER   EDWARD WILMOT

[29]
Memorandum   I HENRY WHITE &t Assign all my right / &t: of this Conveyance unto GEORGE STEPHENS his Heirs &t. for Ever / August the 27th: 1647
Test DANIELL BOUCHER   HENRY WHITE

Memorandum that I GEORGE STEPHENS do for my Exec^{rs} / &t. forever pass over unto THOMAS BOSWELL his Exec^{rs}. &t all my / right & title to this Conveyance as Witness my hand this 26th: / of December 1650
Test JAMES PYLAND   GEORGE STEPHENS
JOHN x PEVERAL

These Three Assignments are Endorsed upon PAWLEYs Conveyance / to WILMOT

     Examined & Truly Transcribed / Test JA^S: BAKER ClCur

Nigh upon the Departure of Mr. ROBERT WATSON out of / this Life this as his Last Will and Testament was the / disposing of his Estate upon the 6th. of November 1651

I Give to JOHN WATSON my Brother Three Thousand pounds / of Tobacco

I give to my Brother JAMES WATSON's Child Two Hundred Acres / of Land after the Decease of my Wife Lying in Pagan Creek / Joyning upon SAM: MATHEWS.

I leave my Wife my Sole Executrix

This was proved to be the Last Will of M[r].: ROBERT WATSON / in open Court at the Isle of Wight County y[e] 9th 9[br]: 1651 by the / Oaths of M[r]. ROBERT DUNSTER Minister & of M[r]. RICHARD / LOCKYER Merchant. Moreover M[rs]. ANN WATSON Relict of / the Said ROBERT Acknowledgeth that he gave the Wife of / TOBY HARST a Cow Caffe and desired her to remember the / youngest Daughter of THO[S]: FLUELLEN

Examined and Truly Transcribed / Test JA[S]: BAKER ClCur

[30]

In the Name of God, Amen. This 14th of / January 1650 I JOHN VASSER the unprofitable servant of God / weak in Body but Strong in mind do willingly and with a / free heart render and give unto the Hands of the Lord my / Creator my Spirit &t. as also my Body in hope of / Resurrection &t. I bestow my Worldly Estate as ffolowith / My Will and pleasure is to Appoint M[r]. JAMES PYLAND and / THOMAS WALTER my overseers of this my Last Will and / Testament over all my Estate. Item. my Will is to give / unto my Eldest Son JOHN VASSER, MILDRED, PETER & ANN / Cows called young Harcus, old Star & young Star / with the female increase of the S[d] Cattle until Such time / they come at age and then them and their Encrease to be / equally Divided amongst them. I give and bequeath unto / my Eldest Daughter ELIZABETH VASSER Two Cows named Brown= / =Bess & Nopus, also a gold ring to be delivered at her day of / Marriage. Lastly. I Give unto my Wife all the / rest of my Whole Estate which I am possest withall / Plantation, Cattle, Hoggs, moveables & Immoveables all within / and abroad, Likewise all Debts and dues by bill bond or / book, making my wife ELIZABETH my Sole Executrix / of all that I am possest withal, this is my last Will / and Testament Witness my hand the day and Year / above Written

Signed Sealed & Delivered   JOHN VASSER Sign[t].
in Psence of
JOHN LEWIS RICHARD AMES TH[O]. WALTER

22

Examined & Truly Transcribed / Test JA^S: BAKER ClCur

In the Name of God, Amen, I JOHN / VALENTINE of the County of the Isle of Wight planter / being Sick and Weak in Body yet ᵱfect in Sence & Memory / do make this my Last Will & Testament in form as ffolloweth / May the Eight 1652

Imprimis: I bequeath my Soul into the hand of Almighty God / who gave it me, most confidently trusting that he will / of

[31]

his infinite mercy through Jesus Christ my Saviour Accept it / and my Body to be Decently Buried in place Convenient as / my Execut^rs: shall think fitt & convenient.

I do Constitute & Appoint my trusty and Welbeloved friends / JOHN MARSHALL and WILLIAM LEWIS of the County aforesaid / Executors or overseers of this my Last Will & Testament / to Se it really & truly performed according to the True / Intent and Meaning thereof without fraud or Deceit / ffor the Land which I am possest withal it is my Will / that it shall be prop^r. to my Eldest Son JAMES VALENTINE / if he Lives till he shall come to the Age of Twenty and One / Years, but if he Shall die before that then my Eldest Daughter / ANN VALENTINE Shall enjoy it. But if she die before She / is married that then my Second Daughter ELIZABETH Shall / enjoy it, And if it shall happen that they shall all die / before they come to perfect age or be Married According / to the P^rmises, that then my youngest Daughter MARGARET / Shall Enjoy it,; [sic] and until such time as these my dear / Children shall come to their full ages, it is my Will that / my Dearly beloved Wife ELIZBETH VALENTINE shall enjoy & / possess to her own prop^r. Use the Said Land during the / time She Shall remain a Widdow without Molestation / of any provided She Keep the Orchard in repair make no more / then Necessary Use of the Timber so that the Land be no ways / unnecessarily destroy'd to the Damage of my Children But if / She Shall Chance to Marry, that then it Shall rest to the discres / =ion of my Overseers to dispose of it to the benefit of my Children / After the discharge of my ffunerall rights, and my Debts paid / I give and bequeath to my Loveing Wife the Third part of / my Estate which Shall be left both of Cattle Chattels and all other / goods Moveable & unmoveable, and the other Two thirds to be / Equally Divided amongst my Children by the rule of proportion, / that is to say, Share & Share alike, the S^d. Estate notwithstanding / to rest in the hands of my Loveing Wife during the time / She Shall remain a Widdow According to the Tennor afores^d. / according to the disposition of my Land to her, my Eldest / Daughter ANN VALENTINE, any thing before Mentioned notwith= / =standing to have no Share nor Claim in the premises Legacies / of

[32]

of the Cattel in regard She hath a Considerable Stock / already Confirmed her, therefore I only give & bequeath / to her at her day of marriage one Cow. And / in Witness of all the afores^d. Premisses I have / hereunto Set my hand the day & year aforesaid

Signed Sealed Subscribed   the marke of JN^O **M** VALENTINE
& Delivered in Psence of
WILL WESTWRAY NICHOLAS NETHERCOAT

Examined & truly Transcribed / Teste JA^S: BAKER ClCur

To all to whome this present Writing shall come / I Lieuten^t. JOHN UPTON Esqr: Send Greeting &c Whereas by / Patent granted to me for Sixteen Hundred Acres of / Land Scituate Lying & being in the Isle of Wight County / in Virginia under the hand of the Hon^bl: S^r: JOHN / HARVEY Knight Governour & Capt: General of Virginia / dated the Tenth of November One Thousand Six / Hundred & Thirty Eight and Sealed with the Seal of the / Colony the fore Mentioned Land belonging to me Know / Know [sic] ye that I the S^d: Lieu^t. Col^o. JOHN UPTON with / Consent of my Loving Wife MARGARETT UPTON for A / Valuable Consideration in hand received, Sold Assigned and / forever Set over unto WILLIAM UNDERWOOD of the Isle of Wight / afores^d: his Heirs Exc^rs: Adm^rs: & Assigns four Hundred Acres / of Land part of the Said patent of Sixteen Hundred / afrs^d: with all Ediffices, Buildings, Erections, & preveledges / belonging to the Same, the S^d. four Hundred Acres of / Land being next Adjoyning to Three Hundred Acres / formerly Sold to ROBERT BRACEWELL Clarke part of the / aforesd. Devidend and to take his Bredth & Length / According to the S^d. Patent; hereby revoking & disclaiming / any Title Challenge or Interest in the S^d. Four Hundred / Acres of Land. Warranting the Justness of my Title / to the S^d. UNDERWOOD his Heirs &t. for Ever against me / My Heirs &t. and against all persons Claiming or

[33]

Pretending title to the same In Witness whereof I the / Said Lieu^t. Col^o. UPTON with my afores^d. Wife have / Set to our hands & Seals this Eighteenth of November / One Thousand Six Hundred fifty & One, And it / is hereupon Agreed that the s^d. UNDERWOOD or his Assigns / Shall pay the Customary Rent due to his Majestie after ye Date of Last / grant Concerning Quitrents

           JOHN UPTON
Signed Sealed and   MARGARETT **M V** UPTON
Deliv^d: in psts. of us

ISAAC CAVALEIR THO^S. SCOTT

Examined and Truly Transcribed / Teste. JA^S BAKER ClCur

Know all men by these psents that I THOMAS / TURNER of the County of Isle of Wight planter, for a Valluable / Consideration to me in hand paid wherewith I acknowledge my / Selfe to be fully Satisfied and paid by these presents Have / Barganed and Sole unto JOHN MOTLY of the Same County / planter, One Hundred Acres of Land Scituate & being in / the County of y^e. Isle of Wight being the moiety of Two Hundred / Acres that was bought of AMBROSE BENNETT between the said / JOHN MOTLY and my Selfe to have and to hold and peaceable / Enjoy the s^d. Hundred Acres of Land with priveledges, freedoms, / Immunities & Immoluments thereunto belonging, thereon being / or therein Included, Furthermore the S^d. TURNER doth / hereby Sell & Assign as afores^d. all Deeds, Charters, Evidences, / Escripts & Writeings which he or any other person or persons / to his use had or have Concerning the Premisses or any parcel / thereof, the said THOMAS TURNER hereby affirming & Warranting / this to be a Lawfull Deed of Sale discharging & Acquitting y^e / Said JOHN MOTLY his Heirs Exec^{rs}: & Adm^{rs}: from all Incumber= / = ances Whatsoever Except the Rent formerly Called the Kings / Rent, Lastly. The said shall at all times & Demands / before the xxiiii of June next after the date Suffer and / Cause to be done any such thing and things as shall / lend to the further Confirmation and Establishment of / the

[34]
Sale unto the Said MOTELY with further Warant / against all Claims whatsoever peaceably to Enjoy the / Same without Lett or hindrance of the S^d. TURNER his / Heirs Exc^{rs}. Or Assigns or any other persons by reason of / any Claim of Title before the date hereof in Witness / of which Bargan Sute covenant, Grant, on the behalf / of the S^d. THOMAS TURNER to be Truly performed, he / doth hereunto Set his hand the 24th. Day of June / One Thousand and Six Hundred & fifty Two.

The mark of
THOMAS |⁻⁻| TURNER

Sealed & Delivered in
the psence of us
SAMUEL NICHOLES FRAN: WHITTINGTON

Examined and Truly Transcribed / Test: JA^S: BAKER ClCur

Know all men by these presents that I Capt. JOHN / UPTON of the Isle of Wight County in Virginia do hereby / for and in Consideration of a Valluable

Summ in / hand received Sell Assign & Confirm unto JOHN / VALLENTINE planter of the Same County his Heirs / and Assigns for Ever, a Certain parcel of Land of / a Hundred Acres of thereabouts being the Land that / THOMAS BUSH formerly held by Pattent which hath / Since fallen into my Survey, In Witness / Whereof I hereunto Sett my hand this 9th. of / January: 1650

JOHN UPTON

Test WILL: UNDERWOOD
The mark **W** of W[M]: LEWES

Vera Record: 9th. Augt: 1652 ꝑ R[l]: W[M]:SON ClCur

Examined & Truly Transcribed / Test JA[S]: BAKER CLCur

[35]

To all to Whome these ꝑsents shall Come I RICH[D]. / KEMP Esq[r]: Govern[r]: & Cap[t]., General of Virginia Send Greeting / in our Lord God Everlasting. Whereas, by Instructions from / the Kings most Excellent Majestie directed to me and the / Council of State, His Majestie was gratiously pleased to / Authorise me the Said Govern[r]: and the Councill to Grant / pattents and to Assign Such proportions of Land to all Advertu= / rers and planters as have been usuall in Such Cases heretofore / either for Adventurers for Money or Transportation of people into / this Colony according to the order of the late Company and Since / allowed by his Majestie, and that the Same Course be Continued / to all adventurers and planters until it shall be otherwise / Determined by his Majistie, Now Know Ye that I / the S[d]: RICHARD KEMP Esq[r]: do with the Concent of the Councill / of State Accordingly give grant and Confirm unto ROBERT / LAURENCE Two Hundred Acres of Land Scituatue [*sic*] & being / on the Eastermost side of Lawnes Creek in the County of the / Isle of Wight, Westerly upon the S[d]. Creek, from thence East by South / Joyning upon M[r]. HARDINGs Lands forty Six pole, from / thence along the Marked Tree of Widdow BENNETT, South / & by West, Two Hundred & Sixty poles, thence West one Hund[d]. / forty Two poles, thence along a Swamp North Eighty Two poles / to the Creek, The S[d]. Two Hundred Acres of Land being due / unto him the S[d]. ROBERT LAURANCE by a former patent / bearing date the five & Twentyeth day of August 1642 and / by and for the Transportation of four persons into the / Colony, whose names are in the records mentioned under / the S[d]. Patent. To Have and to Hold, the said / Two Hundred Acres of Land with his due Share of all / Mines & Minerals therein contained, and with all rights & / privelidges, of Hunting, Hawking, ffishing & ffowling, as / also all woods, waters & Rivers, and all profits Commodities & / Hereditaments whatsoever to the S[d]. Land or any of them / belonging unto the S[d]: ROBERT LAWRENCE his Heirs & Assigns / for Ever in as large and Ample manner to all intents and / purposes as is Expressed in a Charter of orders from the / late Treasurer & Company bearing date the Eighteenth / of November 1618. or by Consequences may be Justly Collected / out

[36]

out of the Same or out of the Letters patent / wherein they are granted, To be held of our Sovereign / Lord the King his Heirs & Successors for Ever as of / his Manner of East Greenwich in free & Common / Soccage, and not in Capite nor by Knights Service / Yeilding and paying unto our Sovereign Lord the King his Heirs and Successors for Ever, for Every fifty / acres of Land herein by these presents given & granted / yearly at the feast of S^t: Michael the Archangel, the fee rent of one Shilling to his Majesties Use, which / payment is to be made Seven years after the Date of / the first patent of the 25th. of August 1642, and not / before, according to the Said Charter of orders from the late / Treasurer & Company & Since Confirmed by his Majesties / Said Instructions, as also by Act of Assembly bearing / date the 6th. of January 1639. Provided always / that if the S^d. ROBERT LAURANCE his Heirs or Assigns / do not Plant & seat or Cause to be planted or Seated on / the s^d. Two Hundred Acres of Land within the time or / term of three years next ensueing the date of these / presents, that then it shall and may be Lawfull / for any Adventurer or Planter to make Choyce and / Seat upon the Same; Given at James City under / my hand & Seal with the Seal of the Colony this / 12th. day of Septemb^r 1644 and in the xxth: year of / the Reign of our Sovereign Lord King Charles &t

RICHARD KEMP

Know all men by these presents that I ROBERT / LAURENCE for me my Heirs and Assigns for a Valuable / Consideration already in hand received, fully and Absolutely / assigns over unto DANIEL WASHBORN his Heirs sand Assigns / for Ever, all my right, Title, & Interest of the Two Hundred / Acres of Land within this patent mentioned. Witness my / hand & Seal this 8th. day of July 1652

the mark

Test ROB^T. SABIN JAMES PYLAND   of ROB^T: **R L** LAURENCE

the seal

Recorded 9th. August 1652

[37]

Examined and Truly Transcribed / test JA^S: BAKER ClCur

In the Name of God, Amen. I / JOHN STILES being Sick, and weak in Body but of perfect / Memory for which I bless and praise the Almighty God, and / my Saviour Jesus Christ, I do make this my Last Will / and Testament (as ffolloweth).

Imprimis, I give and bequeath my Body to the Earth to be decently / Intered therein, and I bequeath my Soul into the hands / of Jesus Christ my most Loveing and Mercifull Saviour / and Redeemer Humbly Beseeching him of his Infinite / Mercy to Pardon and to forgive me all my Sins, and to / present me without Spot and blameless before the Presence / of God his ffather, to whome with the holy Ghost I do Ascribe / from the Ground and Bottom of my Heart, all Honour / and Glory both now and for Evermore; Amen / And, for that Estate the which it hath pleased God of his / Mercy to bestow upon me, my Debts being first paid / I give and bequeath as ffolloweth

Item, I give and Bequeath unto my Son JOHN STILES all my / Plantation being Two Hundred Acres of Land together / with the Cattle hereafter Specified, (Viz^t.) One Brown / Cow called by the Name of Peile, and one Brindle pyde / Cow called by the name of ffortune, and a red Cow with a / bob taile, a pale red Cow called by the name of Rose, and / one Whiteish brown pyed Heifer about three years old, and one / blackish Cow Calfe white aboute the udder and about the / hinder feet, and one Cow Calfe of a red Colour which Two / Calves were fallen this past year, All which Cattle being Seven in number I do give unto my Son JOHN STILES with all their / increase both mail & female, as also I give unto my Son / JOHN STILES One Grisled Sow Shoate About half a year old

Item, I give unto JOHN MURRY my Godson One Cowcafe [*sic*] / to be paid the next Ensueing Year

Item, I give unto ELIZABETH JOHNSON my Goddaughter one / Cow calfe to be paid Two years hence.

Item, I give unto JOANE MADDIN my Goddaughter One / Cowcalfe to be paid Three Years hence

[38]

Item I give and bequeath all the remainder of my / Estate, whether Cattel, Hoggs, Household Stuff, Servants / Debts, or any other thing to mee belonging, or anywise / appertaining unto my Loveing Wife ELIZABETH STILES / and do make her my full & whole Execut^x: of this / my Last Will & Testament.

Item I do desire my Loveing friend HUMPHREY / CLARK to be my Overseer to Se this my Last / Will & Testament pformed & fullfilled, And in / Witness of the Truth hereof I have hereunto set / my hand & Seal this 26th. of Octob^r: 1652

Being present   Sig.

THOMS [*sic*] JOHNSON   JOHN S STILES

JAMES PYLAND

Record: 9th. Novr: 1652 / Examined & Truly Transcribed / Teste: JA[S]. BAKER ClCur

In the Name of God , Amen. I Cap[t]. / JOHN UPTON of the Isle of Wight County in Virginia / Gent, being Sick of Body but in perfect Memory do / Ordinan this my Last Will and Testament in Manner / and form as followeth (that is to Say) ffirst I commit my / Body to the Earth from whence it came to be decently / Interred at the discression of my Executrix hereafter in / these psents mentioned. And my Soul to God hopeing for / Salvation through the Merritts of my Lord & Saviour / Jesus Christ, and for Such worldly Goods as God in his / Mercy hath bestowed upon me I bequeath and Devise in / Manner & fforme ffollowing, Imprimis, Item. / I give Devise & bequeath unto my Eldest Son JOHN / UPTON all that Tract of Land being part of it in the / Tenure of JOHN KING, JAMES BAGNALL, & NICHOLAS / MORRIS, Containing in the Whole Eight Hundred and / fifty Acres of Land, and if the Said JOHN UPTON / dies before he Comes to the Age of One and Twenty / years then I give and bequeath the Said Land unto / WILLIAM

[39]

WILLIAM, ELIZABETH, SARAH & MARGARETT UNDERWOOD to be / Divided as followeth (Viz[t]) ELIZABETH, SARAH & MARGARETT / UNDERWOOD each of them A Hundred Acres, and the / remainder unto WILLIAM UNDERWOOD, Item I Give and / bequeath unto my said Son one Mare fole, and one Cow / with Calfe, being upon the Probate of my Will sett apart / for him with their Increase, And if it shall happen that / my said Son dies before the age of one and Twenty then / the s[d] Mare fole and Cow with their Increase to be Equally / Shared amongst my Daughters in Law ELIZABETH, SARAH, & / MARGARETT UNDERWOOD, Item I give and bequeath unto / WILLIAM UNDERWOOD, ELIZABETH, SARAH & MARGARETT / UNDERWOOD, that tract or parcel of Land running upon / this Side the Threshett [sic, "freshet"] near AMBROSE BENNETTs Containing / ffifteen Hundred Acres of Land Except and always reserved / out of this Land Three Hundred Acres which M[r]: ROBERT / BRACEWELL hath. Item, I give and bequeath unto WILLIAM / ELIZABETH, SARAH and MARGARETT UNDERWOOD all my Land / at Rappahannock or what shall be hereafter made good upon my rights / they to be possest with it after my Wife's decease, And / for the rest of my Estate, Goods Chattels, Servants, Household Stuff, Lands / Tenem[ts]: Hereditam[ts]: whatsoever here in Virginia or else / where, after my Debts, Legacies and funeral rights paid & / discharg'd, I give Devise and bequeath the Same unto my / very Loveing and Welbeloved Wife MARGARETT UPTON / whome I constitute, ordain, & make Sole Executrix of this / my Last Will and Testament, and I do heartily desire and / make my Loveing friends M[a]: GEORGE FFAWDON WILLIAM / UNDERWOOD and JAMES TAYLOR Clark, my overseers desiring / them to Se this my Will performed, Likewise I give and / ordain my Execut[x]. to give each of my Overseers a ring of / Twenty shillings Sterling price, Likewise ordain ANN / WILLIAMSON the Wife of JAMES WILLIAMSON to be Equall / Sharer in my Land at Rappahannock with these above / named, Item, I give unto ELIZABETH UNDERWOOD / one pillion & pillion Cloth to be delivered at her / day of Marriage. Furthermore I do by these psents / revoke all former Wills by me made Except this my / Last

[40]

Last Will In Witness, I the said Cap[t]. JOHN / UPTON, have hereunto Set my hand and Seal this / Sixteenth day of January Anno Domoni [--] / It is to be understood that what Land I have formerly dispos'd / of in that Trackt of ffifteen Hundred Acres / upon the frishett by AMBROS BENNETTs is to rest / upon Condition, and the remainder Divided as is / before provided

Sealed & Signed in the   JOHN UPTON Sign[m].
presence of us
JOHN GATLIN's mark JAMES TAYLOR

     This Will was proved in Court the 16th: of Decemb[r]: / Anno 1652 by oaths of WILLIAM UNDERWOOD and EDWARD / SKINNER Record[d]: 16th Decemb[r]: 1652

     Examined and Truly Transcribed / Test JA[S]: BAKER ClCur

     Know all men by these presents that I MARGRET / UPTON Widdow in behalf of my Self my Heirs Ex[rs]: Adm[rs]: / and assigns for and in Consideration of y[e] performance of Two Bills / Amounting to the Value of Two Thousand and Two Hundred / pounds of Tobacco and Cask have given & Granted and / by these presents do give and grant unto JOHN BUTCHER his / heirs Exec[rs] Adm[rs] and Assigns, To Have Hold possess / And Enjoy a Neck of Land whereon now JOHN / ASKWE liveth lying Scituate or being Amongst or / betwixt that Tract of Land which Cap[t]. JOHN BATTS / bought of Cap[t]. JOHN UPTON, the deceased husband / of the Abovementioned M[rs]: MARGARETT UPTON / and disjoined from the Same by Two Swamps / bounded on the Northside with that piece of Land / whereon M[r]. SYMONS old house Standeth, and on / the Southside with a Neck of Land Comonly called / Rowlands Neck, with housing and all appartinancs / thereunto belonging freely to be possessed by the / said JOHN BUTCHER his Heirs Exc[rs]: or Assigns / without Lett or Molestation from the day of the / Date hereof unto the Worlds end be the said / JOHN

[41]

JOHN BUTCHER his Exec^{rs}: or Assigns paying unto the / Said M^{rs}: MARGARETT UPTON her Adm^{rs}: Ex^s. or Ass^{ns}. / the Yearly Acknowledgment of Two Capons, In / Witness whereof I have hereunto set my hand / and Seal this Third day of ffebruary Anno Dom. 1651

Signed & Sealed & Delivered   MARGARETT **MV** UPTON
in the Psence of   markes   Sig^r.
JAMES TAYLOR EDWARD SKYNNER.

Record: primi die Novembr:[6] 1652 / ꝑ RICH: W^M.SON Cl Cur

Exam^d. And Truly Transcribed / Test JA^S: BAKER Cl Cur

Know all Men by these presents that I MARGRETT / UPTON of the Isle of Wight County in Virginia Widdow / late Wife of the deceased Lieuten^t. Col^o. JOHN UPTON / of the Same County Esqr. for divers good Causes and / Considerations me thereunto moveing, have given & granted / and by these presents do give and grant unto PHILLIP / DEWELL of the Said County Planter, all that part or parcell / of Land whereupon the s^d: DEWELL now liveth containing / by Estimation, One Hundred Acres of Land be it / more or less, Scituate lying and being in the aforesaid County / Abutting East upon the Creek called the Pagan Creek Beginning / at a great Swamp adjoyning to the Lands late belonging to / JOHN SPARKS deceased, and now in the Tenure of and / Occupation of JAMES WATSON runing west into the woods / and South abutting upon the Said Creek as the Same is / bounded out with marked trees, together with all proffitts / and Commodities to the s^d. parcell of Land belonging or / Appertaining, To have and to Hold every part and / parcell of the s^d. Lands before mentioned unto the s^d. / PHILIP DEWELL, his Heirs Exec^{rs}: Adm^{rs}: and Assigns / and to his and their proper Use and behoofe for / Ever, And I the s^d. MARGARETT UPTON do hereby / Covenant

[42]

Covenant promisse and grant to and with the said / PHILIP DEWELL his Heirs Exec^{rs}: Adm^{rs}: and Assigns by these / p^{r}sents, That he the s^d. PHILIP DEWELL his Heirs Exec^{rs}: / Adm^{rs}: and Assigns Shall quietly and peaceable Enjoy / the sd. parcell of Land hereby given and granted / without any Lett, Molestation or Contradiction of me / my Heirs Exec^{rs}. or Assigns or any other person or persons / whatsoever by my or their means consent or procure= / =ment for Ever, In

---

[6] "Recorded on the first day of November...."

Witness whereof I have hereunto / Sett my hand & Seal this 9th. day of April Anno Dom / 1652

y[e] marke of

MARGARETT **M V** UPTON

Signed Sealed & Delivered
In the presence of
EDWARD SKYNNER WILLIAM MOSELEY

Record[d]: 9th. ffebr[ij]: 1652 / Exam[d] and Truly Transcribed / Test JA[s] BAKER Cl Cur.

This Indenture made the last day of / July Anno Domini 1652 Betweer JOHN / SWEET on the One party and FFRANCIS ENGLAND on the / othei party Witnesseth that I the said JOHN / SWEET for a valuable Consideratior received of him / the said FFRANCIS ENGLAND do for me my Heirs / Exec[n] Adm[rs] & Assigns Ratify Confirm Avouch and / and by these P[r]sents for ever pass over unto him the / said FFRANCIS ENGLAND his Heirs Ex[rs] Adm[rs] & Assigns / four Hundred & fifty Acres of Land scituate lying / being in the Isle of Wight County ffour Hundred / Acres of the said Land lying and being at the / Eastermost Branch of Blackwater being the outmost Southerly / Bounds and N: W. & by W. upon the said Branch of / Blackwater which Land is part of ffifteen Hundred / and forty acres of Land taken up by the s[d] JN[O] SWEET

[43]
according to the Patent of the s[d] JOHN SWEET to which / relation being had more fully at large appeareth And / the other ffifty acres of Land lying and being next / adjoining to the Land of FFRANCIS ENGLAND and North / on the Lands of Captain PEARCE at y[e] other end of / the said Land To have and to Hold / all & singular the s[d] four Hundred & fifty Acres of Land / with all due share of Mines & Minerals therein / contained and with all Rights profits & Commodities / thereunto belonging or any ways appertaining unto him / the sd FFRANCIS ENGLAND his Heirs Executors Adm[rs] & Assigns / for ever in as large & ample manner to all Intents / & purposes as expressed in a Letter of Orders from / the late Treasurer & Company bearing date y[e] 18th of Nov[r]: 1618 as in and by y[e] s[c] SWEET his Patent / bearing date at James City the 26 day of September / 1645 more at large appeareth To be Held of our / Sovereign Lord the King his Heirs & Successors and / of his Mannor of East Greenwich in free and / common Soccage and not in Capite or by Knights / Service Yeilding & Paying unto the Keepers ol the / Common wealth of England for Their rent Gatherers / for the s[d] ffour Hundred & fifty Acres of Land / the Sum of nine Shillings Sterling at the ffeast / of S[t]. Michael the Arch Angel as in & by the / s[d] JOHN SWEET his Patent

whereunt[o] relation being had / more at large appeareth In Witness whereof y^e / s^d JOHN SWEET have interchangeably set my Hand & / Seal ye day & Year first above written
Sealed Signed & Delivered   JOHN SWEET (Seal)
JAMES PYLAND. THO^S. WOODWARD

       Examined & truly Transcribed / Teste JA^S: BAKER ClCur

[44]
       This is the last Will & Testament of me JOSEPH / COBBS Aged Sixty Years of Age or thereabouts / Imprimis I do Bequeath unto my well beloved / Wife ELIZABETH COBBS one parcel of Land containing / Three Hundred Acres of Land or thereabout commonly / called Goose Hill Land And further I do / Bequeath unto my well beloved Wife all Movables / that are upon the s^d Land, as Cattle (to say) / Seventeen head of Cows & Yearlings and three / Calves with Hoggs Young & Old Thirty two or / thereabouts. Provided she does Marry, ye said / Children that are left shall have Each a Childs / Proportion and so to be divided between them / And further I do Bequeath to my Son BENJAMIN / COBBS one red Cow and her Calf. Item and further / I do Bequeath to my Son PHAROAH COBBS one Cow / and her Calf red. Item and further I do / Beaqueath unto my Daughter ELIZABETH COBBS one / black Cow and one black Yearling Item this / is my last Will & Testament now living at the Mercy / of God in my Death Bed in good Sense As / Witness my Hand this 1st day of March / Anno Dom: 1653
Signed Sealed and   JOSEPH **E** COBBS (Seal)
Deliv^d in ye Presence of
Us
JOSEPH DUNN JN^O CHELD

       Exm^d & truly Transcribed / Teste JA^S: BAKER ClCur

[45]
       This Indenture made the last day of / September Anno Dom 1652 Between CHRISTOPHER / LEWIS of the one party and JOHN BURGESS on the other pty / Witnesseth that I the said CHRISTOPHER LEWIS do / firmly by these presents for me my Heirs Exe^{cts} Adm^{rs} and / Assigns ratify and confirm avouch and for ever pass / over unto him The said JOHN BURGESS his Exec^{rs} Adm^{rs} / and Assigns one piece and parcel of Land containing / by estimation Two Hundred Acres of Land be it more / or less scituate lying & being in James Town County / at a Placed called by the Name of Blackwater on the Western / side of that Swamp and being bounded South on the Land / of JAMES PYLAND North

33

on the Land of THO^S. TABERER / & FFRANCIS HIGGENS West into the Woods and y^e Easterly / Bounds to begin at the Mains Swamp To have and / to Hold all & singular the said Two Hundred Acres / of Land with all due share of Mines & Minerals therein / contained and with all Rights profits & Commodities there= / unto belonging or any ways appertaining unto him the / said JOHN BURGESS his Heirs Executors Adm^{rs} & Assigns / for ever in as large & ample manner to all Intents and / Purposes as is expressed in a Charter of Orders from the / late Directors & Company bearing date the 18th November / 1618 as in and by the sd XROPHER LEWIS his Patent / bearing date at James City the 4th of July 1649 / more at large appeareth To be held of our Sovereign / Lord the King his Heirs & Successors as of his Mannor / of East Greenwich in free & common Soccage not in / Capite nor Knights Service Yeilding & Paying / unto the Keepers of the Common Wealth of England / or their Rent gatherers for the said Two hundred / Acres of Land the Sum of ffour Shillings Sterling / at the ffeast of S^t. Michael the Arch Angel as in and by / the s^d CHRISTOPHER LEWIS his Patent whereunto relation

[46]

being had more at large appeareth And further / I the said CHRISTOPHER LEWIS do bind me my Heirs Ex^{rs} / and Assigns from Time to Time and at all times to / Warrant the s^d Land unto him the s^d JOHN BURGESS / and his Assigns from any person whatsoever which shall / lay any claim thereunto according to Patent In / Witness whereof I the said CHRISTOPHER LEWES / have hereunto interchangeable set my Hand & Seal / the Day and Year first above written
Sealed and Delivered
In presence of Us   CHRISTOP^R: **C** LEWIS (Seal)
JA^S PYLAND RICHD SHARP TH^O: **T W** WARNER

Exm^d and truly Transcribed / Test JA^S: BAKER ClCur

In the Name of God Amen / the first day of May 1654. I CHRISTOPHER REYNOLDES / of the Isle of Wight County in Virginia Plantor / being healthful in Body and sound in Mind & Memory / make this my Last Will & Testament in manner / and form as followeth. First I give and / bequeath my Soul into the Hands of God my Creator / and Maker and my Body to be Buried in sure / and certain Hope of Resurection to Eternal Lyfe / thro' the only Merit & Satisfaction of Jesus Xt / my only Saviour & Reedemer. Imprimis / I give & Bequeath unto my Son CHRISTOPHER REYNOLDS / all my Land on the Southerly side of the / freshet Swamp that RICHARD JORDAN now liveth / upon, And I give unto my Son JOHN all my / Land on the Northerly side of the said freshet

[47]
Swamp and one Cow and he to enjoy the said Land / at Twenty one Years of Age. And unto my Son / RICHARD I give all my Land I now live upon / and one Cow and he to possess the s^d Land / at Twenty one Years of Age. And my Daughter / ABBASHA I have given unto her a Portion already / which was two Cows and two Calves. And I / Give unto my daughter ELIZABETH one Heifer of / two Years old besides the Stock I gave her / formerly. And unto my Daughter JANE I give / one Cow and one Yearling Heifer. And I Give / unto GEORGE RIVERS one Yearling Heifer And / I give unto the Child my Wife now goeth with / if it lives two Cows to enjoy them at three / Years old. And if any of my Children dye / my Will is that the other should Succeed what / Estate they leave. And unto ELIZABETH my / loving Wife I give all the rest of my Estate / both Goods & Chattels Movable & Unmovable and / Debts that are due to me from any person or persons / whatsoever and my two Servants she paying / all my Debts truly & justly. And I do Constitute / and Ordain ELIZABETH my loving Wife my whole / & sole Executrix. And my Will is that my / Wife ELIZABETH shall have the ordering & bringing / up JOHN & RICHARD my Sons until they be / sixteen Years of Age, and ELIZABETH & JANE / until they be fifteen Years of Age. In / Witness whereof I the s^d CHRISTOPHER REYNOLDS / have hereunto set my Hand & Seal the Day & Year / first above written
Sealed Subscribed

CHRIS^R: REYNOLDS (Seal)

Turn over

[48]
Sealed Subscribed and Delivered
In the Presence of
SYLVESTER **B** BULLEN ANTHONY **A** MATHEWS

Examined and truly Transcribed / Teste JA^S: BAKER ClCur

In the name of God. Amen / November this 24: 1656. I JOSHUATH TABERNER [sic] / being of whole Mind and good & perfect Memory / Laud & Praise Almighty God make & ordain this / my last Will & Testament concerning herein my /last Will in manner & form following that is to / say First I commend my Soul unto Almighty / God & Maker and Redeemer and my Body to be / Buried at the Discretion of my Brother, and after / my Debts paid and my ffuneral Expences pformed / the Remainder I bequeath as followeth. I Give / and queath [sic] to my Brother THOMAS TABERNER / all such Houses Lands

Money or Chattels Movables / or Immoveables as shall any way appear due to me / either as a portion given of left me by the last / Will & Testament of my Father WILLIAM TABERER / of the County of Darby or otherwise appertaining / or belonging unto me with all profit thereof / during his natural Life he my aboves^d Brother / THOMAS bestowing as a Legacy to my Brother / WILLIAM TABERER of the County of Derby and / the rest of my Fathers Kindred Ten Pounds Sterling / or the Value thereof out of my s^d Estate in

[49]

England. And my Will is that after my Brother / THOMAS his decease, his only Daughter & Heir / RUTH TABERER be possessed with all my foresaid / Estate in England as my only Heir & Executrix / to her & heirs for ever Also I give my / Cousin RUTH TABERER all my female Cattle in / Virginia being four in Number of my owne / mark to her & Heirs for ever, and the Remainder / of my whole Estate in Virginia I give to my / Brother THOMAS TABERER and further in Case / of denyal I give my Brother THOMAS TABERER / full power to Sue and by Law to Recover my / s^d Estate in England and to see it disposed of / according to the Tennor of this my Will / And that this my Will may be valid and / effectual in Law according to the Intent and / purpose I confirm it with my Hand and / Seal the Day and Year first above written

Signed Sealed and   JOSHUA TABERER / (Seal)
Delivered in the Presence of Us
WILLIAM LEWER FFRANS: HIGGENS

          Examined & truly Transcribed / Teste JA^S: BAKER ClCur

[50]

          Whereas a Patent was granted by S^r. WILLIAM / BERKLEY Governour &c under the Colony Seal dated / the 19th April 1648 unto JOHN KING & LAWRENCE WARD / for ffive hundred Acres of Land scituate or being in / the County of the Isle of Wight and lying on the / head of a Branch of the Pagan Bay Creek called / the ffreshett and beginning at a marked Hickory / standing on a Hill called Turkey Hill and running / West by South Two Hundred twenty five Pole crossing / The said ffreshett unto a marked red Oak and so / South Three hundred Twenty pole unto a marked red / Oak and so East by North Two hundred Twenty / five Pole unto a marked red Oak standing by / a Pond and so N:N:E. one Hundred eighty Pole / unto a Gum and so N.N:W. unto the first mentioned / marked Tree &c which foresaid JOHN KING being deced / the aboves^d LAWRENCE WARD conveyeth his Right / unto KINGs Wife by an Indorsement on the Patent / in these Words (viz) These presents / Justify that I LAWRENCE WARD do assign / all my Right & Title of this Patent to / M^{rs}. ELIZABETH KING Widdow as Witness / my hand the 14th of May 1655

Witness THO^S: DAVIS ꝑ me   LAWRENCE WARD

Exm^d and truly Transcribed / Teste JA^S: BAKER ClCur

[51]

     Know all Man by these presents that / I GEORGE LOBB of Mulberry Island in Virginia Gent / do Alienate Bargain Sell and Enfeoff Assign and make over all my Right Title & Interest in three / Hundred Acres of Land lying in Stanley Hundred / granted unto me by Patent dated the 12th of / March 1653 unto JOHN BREWER of the Isle of / Wight County Gent his Heirs Exec^{rs} Adm^{rs} or Assigns / for ever for and in Consideration of Three Thousand / Pound of good Tobacco & Cask the which I do / Acknowledge to have received before the Signing & / deliverey hereof and do Oblidge me my Heirs Exec^{rs} / and Administrators to save defend & keep harmless / the said BREWER his Heirs Executors Administrators / from any Person or Persons that shall any wise / lay Claim to the said Three Hundred Acres of Land / or any part or parcel of the same In Witness / whereof I the said LOBB hath hereunto set my / Hand & Seal this 9th day of December 1656

GEORGE LOBB (Seal)

Sealed & delivered
In ye Presence of
THO^S: PRITCHARD JN^O SMITH JAMES PYLANDE

Exm^d and truly Transcribed / Teste JA^S: BAKER ClCur

[52]

     To all true Christian People to whom this / present Writing shall come ** [written in the left-hand margin] I JOHN PAWLEY of Virginia Surgeon send Greeting in our Lord God Everlasting Now know ye that I the s^d ** JOHN PAWLEY on / the Day of the Date hereof hath Exchanged with RICHARD / ATKINS a parcel of Land And I the said JOHN PAWLEY / doth give unto the said RICHARD ATKINS his Heirs / Executors Adm^{rs} & Assigns the Fee Simple of Two / Hundred Acres of Land for One (Viz) being at / the Head of Lawnes Creek bending North upon / THOMAS STAMP East upon the Mill South upon / a fresh Water Swamp and west into the Woods / along the said Swamp running from the Mill one / Mile and three Quarters wanting ten Pole And / I the said JOHN PAWLEY for me my Heirs Executors / Administrators Assigns do freely clearly and / Absolutely deliver unto the said RICHARD ATKINS / his Heirs Executors Administrators & Assigns the / aforesd Two Hundred Acres of Land in ffee Simple / for ever And the said JOHN PAWLEY for him his / Heirs Executors Administrators & Assigns doth / Covenant to and with the said

RICHARD his Heirs / Executors Administrators & Assignes that he and they / shall peaceable & quietly Have Hold Occupy / Possess & Enjoy all and singular the said Land / with the Appurtenances thereunto belonging to him / the af^c RICHARD ATKINS his Heirs Executors Adm^{rs} / and Assigns for ever with his due share of all / Mines & Minerals therein contained mentioned / and expressed and also his Priviledge for ffishing / Hawking ffowling & Hunting within the

[53]

Precincts before specified and that in as large ample / and effectual manner to all Intents & Purposes as it / is granted to me. In witness whereof I have / hereunto set my Hand & Seal this 29th day of May Anno Dom / 1644

Sealed & Delivered   JOHN: PAWLEY (Seal)
In the presence of Us
EUSTACE GRIMES ROB^T: PARKES

       Memorandum that I RICHARD ATKINS do / assign over all my Right & Title herein specified / unto THOMAS WEBB or his Assigns Witness my Hand / this 12th of June 1645

                          RICHARD ATKINS
Teste DANIEL BOUCHER HENRY **H** WHITE

       Examined & truly Transcribed / Teste JA^S: BAKER ClCur

       To all to whom this present Writing shall come / Know Ye that We ELIZABETH & PHAROAH COBBS of / the County of Isle of Wight in Virginia hath for many / considerable Causes Us thereunto moving sold unto / SAMUEL HASWELL of the County aforesd one Piece or parcel / of Land whereon he now Liveth being bounded by / several marked Trees at the Head of the s^d Land / formerly held by Lease to the s^d HASWELL and never / enlarged upon the Sale hereof in the Breadth to a / great Poplar Tree standing by the now cleared plantation / of We the af^d. ELIZABETH & PHAROAH COBBS for which Land / with the Bounds & Limmitts now held by the s^d HASWELL / We do by these P^{r}sents acknowledge to have received

[54]

full Satisfaction also by these binding ourselves / and either of Us our Heirs Executors & Adm^{rs} / or either of them to give to the s^d HASWELL his / Heirs Executors Adm^{rs} or Assigns such secure / Assurance for the said Land with all thereunto / belonging that he and they shall peaceably & / quietly Enjoy the same to him and his Heirs / for ever In Witness whereof we have / Hereunto set our Hands & Seals this 7th day / of March 1656

Signed   ELIZABETH x COBBs

In Presence of Us   PHAROAH x COBBS
JN^O. CORDWENT THO^S GORDONE

Acknowledged in Court by ELIZABETHE / COBBS Attorney, and by
PHAROAH COBBS in Person / The 9° July 1657, et eadem Die Recordatur[7]

Exam^d and truly Transcribed / Teste JA^S: BAKER ClCur

[55]

Know ye all Men by these presents that I / WILLIAM YARRETT &
MARGARET my Wife of the / Isle of Wight County in Virginia Have Given /
Granted Bargained Sold Enfeoffed & Confirmed / and by these presents do for us
our Heirs Executors / and Adm^rs clearly & absolutely Give Grant Bargain / Sell
Enfeoff & Confirm unto ROBERT BIRD & SUSANNAH / his Wife of the same
County their Heirs Executors / or Assigns all the Land lying on ye Westerside / of
Goose-hill Creek which did belong to a Patent / of Seven Hundred Acres of Land
which was in Co / partnership between me and HUGH WINN deced / but since
by vertue of a Partition or Division / made between me and The s^d WINN solely
appertaining / to my part which Land so Alienated by me and / my Wife is in
Consideration and Exchange of a / parcel of Land lying on ye Easterside of y^e
head / of Goose-hill Creek & Swamp which did belong / unto a Patent for One
Hundred fifty Acres of Land / which I the s^d YARRETT & HUGH WINN sold
unto / The said BIRD and is since renewed in ye s^d BIRDs / own Name To have
and to Hold / the said Land af^d on the Westerside of Goosehill Creek / with all
Liberties & Priviledges whatsoever (mentioned / more at large in the Patent) to
him the s^d ROBERT / BIRD & SUSANNA his Wife their Heirs Executors /
Adm^rs & Assigns for ever without the Lett hindrance / Suit Molestation or
Disturbance of Use our Heirs / Executors Administrators or Assigns or any other
/ person or persons Claiming by from or under Us / In Witness and Confirmation
whereof we / have hereunto set our Hands and Seals
Turn over

[56]

this fourth day of July in the Year of our / Lord One Thousand Six Hundred fifty
& Seven   W^M: **W** YARRETT (Seal)
Signed Sealed & Dl^d   MARGARET YARRETT (Seal)
in presence of Us
W^M BRACEY THO^S WOODWARD

---

[7] "And recorded on the same day."

Acknow[d] in Court by WILLIAM YARRETT & his Wife / the 9th July 1657 Et eadem Die recordatur / Exam[d] and truly Transcribed / Teste JA[S] BAKER ClCur

Know all Men by these presents that / I ROBERT BIRD and SUSANNA my Wife of the Isle / of Wight County in Virginia Have Given and / Granted Bargained Sold Enfeoffed & Confermed and / by these presents do for us our Heirs Exec[rs] & Adm[rs] / clearly & absolutely Give Grant Bargain Sell Enfeoff / and Confirm unto WILLIAM YARRETT & MARGARET his / Wife of the same County their Heirs Exec[rs] or / Assigns all the Land lying on the Easterside of / the Head of Goose-hill Creek & Swamp which did / belong unto a Patent for One Hundred fifty Acres / of Land which I the s[d] ROBERT BIRD bought of / The said WILLIAM YARRETT & HUGH WINN and is since / renewed in my own Name which said Land so / Alienated by me and my Wife is in Consideration / and Exchange of a parcel of Land lying on the / Westerside of Goose-hill Creek which did belong to / a Patent of Seven Hundred Acres of Land

[57]
which was in Copartnership between the said W[M] YARRETT & / HUGH WINN deceased but since by vertue of a Partition or / Division made between them solely appertaining to the / said YARRETTs part To have and to Hold / the sd Land afores[d] on the Easterside of Goose hill Creek / and Swamp with all Liberties & priviledges whatsoever / mentioned more at large in the Patent to him the / s[d] WILLIAM YARRETT & MARGARET his Wife their Heirs Exec[rs] / Adm[rs] & Assigns for ever without the Lett hindrance / Suit Molestation or Disturbance of Use our Heirs / Executors Adm[rs] or Assigns or any other person or persons / Claiming by from or under us In Witness and / Confirmation whereof we have hereunto set our Hand / and Seals this fourth day of July in the Year of / our Lord One thousand six hundred fifty & seven

Signed Sealed & Deliv[d]   ROB[T] **R B** BIRD
in the p[r]sence of Us   SUSANNA **S** BIRD
W[M]: BRACEY THO[S]: WOODWARDE

Exam[d] and truly Transcribed / Test JA[S]: BAKER ClCur

Whereas by Patent dated the 4[th] June 1655 / there was granted unto JARVASE DODSON six hundred / acres of Land in the County of Lancaster bounding / N: E[dly] upon a Branch of Corotomen River and upon / the Land of one HAWKES including the head of the / said Branch S: E[dly] upon the Land of W[M] THACKER / S: W[dly] and N: W[dly] upon the main Woods, which said / patent & Land y[e] s[d] DODSON assigneth by Writing / under his Hand at y[e] ffoot of y[e] said Patent unto THOMAS

[58]

HARRIS in these Words. These Presents / Witness that I JARVASE DODSON for and in / Consideration of ffour Thousand and eight Hundred / pounds of good sound Merchantable Tobacco & Cash to / be paid upon Demand in places Convenient at / Rapahannock on Potomac River do hereby sell / and Assign over all my Right Title & Interist / to and in the above s^d Patent and Land from / me and my Heirs to THOMAS HARRIS his Heirs or / Assigns for ever and engage to Warrant that / I have good Right to make a firm and lawfull / Sale thereof To have and to Hold / the said Land to him the said THOMAS HARRIS his / Heirs or Assigns for ever in as full & ample / manner as it is by the sd Patent granted / For the full Confirmation whereof I have hereunto / set my Hand this 4 ffeb 1656.

Witness: JER: DODSON
JOHN SHARP, HOWEL POWELL

These Presents Witness that / I JARVASE DODSON do hereby Constitute & Appoint / my loving ffriend Capt FFRANCIS HOBBS my true / and lawful Attorney for me and in my Name / to acknowledge in Court the Sale of Six Hundred / Acres of Land as may now at large appear by / my Sale & Assignment given under my hand / under ye Patent herewith delivered to my said / friend Captain HOBBS for ye Use of THOMAS / HARRIS of the Isle of Wight County and I / acknowledge to have received the Quantity of / ffour Thousand and eight Hundred pounds

[59]

of Tobacco and Cask of the said Captain HOBBES / for the Use of the said THOMAS HARRIS according to / agreement upon ye sd Sale wherewith I am fully / Contented & Satisfied Therefore have I hereby / authorised my s^d loving ffriend Capt HOBBES / my lawful Attorney as afores^d to acknowledge / the same in Court and do hereby bind my / Self my Heirs Exec^{rs} or Adm^{rs} to ratify and / Confirm what my said Attorney shall do / therein according to Law As Witness / my Hand this 5 day of Feb: 1656

Witness   JAR: DODSON
ANDREW BOZER W^M w THATCHER

These Presents Witness that I / WILLIAM THATCHER Planter in Corotoman River in ye County / of Lancaster have made & ordained and by these / P^{r}sents do Constitute Authorise & Appoint and put / in my Stead & place my Loving & kind ffriend / Capt FFRANCS HOBBS living in the Isle of Wight County / in James River to be my true & lawful Attorney / to acknowledge &

confess the Right of Seven Hundred / and fifty Acres of Land sold by the afores[d] WILLIAM / THATCHER to THOMAS HARRIS planter in the Isle of Wight / County in James River and upon Confession of the said / Right of Land to ask demand & receive of the said / HARRIS all such Debts Deeds & Demands, as are / due owing or belonging to me from the said

[60]

HARRIS by any manner of ways or means whatsoever / Giving and hereby Granting to my s[d] Attorney the / full power & Authority of my Self as well for the / receiving recovering & getting of the Premise or any / of them as also for the acquitting & discharging him / the said HARRIS thereof Satisfaction being Given / for the same so and in such manner as my said / Attorney shall see fitt or expedient to be done in or / about the P[r]misses and any of them and all and / singular they to stand in verulant fforce and in as / ample manner as I my self might or could do were / I perssonaly present holding firm & stable all / and whatsoever my said Attorney shall so do or cause / to be done In Witness whereof the said WILLIAM / THATCHER have hereunto set my Hand this 19th day of / November Anno 1656

Test EDWARD BYHAM   W[M] x THATCHER
ROBERT **R G** GRAVES

By Virtue of this Power I do Oblidge my / Self to Procure a Patent of Two Hundred Acres of / Land bounding upon Six Hundred Acres of Land / granted to JARVASE DODSON by Patent dated / 4th June 1655 Witness my hand this 10th August / 1657

FRANCIS HOBBS

Exam[d] and truly Transcribed
Test JA[S] BAKER ClCur

[61]

Be it known unto all Men by / These Presents that I THOMAS TABERER Of the Isle of / Wight County Attorney of NICHOLAS GEORGE of the / County of Lancaster have in the behalf of the said / GEORGE and my Self Bargained & Sold and do forever / Alienate Bargain & Sell unto FFRANCIS AYERS of the / Isle of Wight County his Heirs Executors Administrators / or Assigns the full & whole Right Title Claim or / Interist that we have of Nine Hundred Acres of Lande / lying upon Blackwater and by patent given unto / NICHOLAS GEORGE THOMAS TABERER and HUMPHRY CLARK / And I do further bind my self in the Behalf of / the aboves[d] NICHOLS GEORGE and for my self to make / such farther Assurance of the said Land unto / FFRANCIS AYRES his Heirs Executors or Assigns as shall / be requisite or required

lawfully at the Coast and / Charge of the said FFRANFCIS AYRES Witness / my Hand this 28th day of February 1656
Signed in P^rsence of Us   THO^S TABERER
ROBERT **R B** BIRD
THOMAS **T**: **L**: LEWIS

Exm^d and truly Transcribed / Test JA^S: BAKER ClCur

[62]
This Indenture made this Eighth day / of March Anno Domini One Thousand six hundred fifty & / Five Between MARGARET UPTON Rilict and / Administratrix of Lieu^t Col^o JOHN UPTON decd lately of / the Isle of Wight County of the one party and / FFRANCIS SLAUGHTER of the same County Gent on / the other party Witnesseth that Whereas the / said Lieu^t Col^o JOHN UPTON in his Life time made / sale of a parcel of Land lying in the said County to / Capt. JOHN BATT formerly made over as a / Jointure or Dowry to ffeoffees in Trust for the / Use & Claim of the said MARGARET UPTON as by the / S^d. Deed more at large may appear And Whereas / also the honourable Governour & Council of Virginia / by Order of Court dated at James City the / 29th of November 1652 in Retaliation and making / good the value of the said Dowry so illegally / Alienated from the said MARGARET & Administra^x / of the said L^t: Col^o JOHN UPTON according to the / Value of the Consideration from the s^d BATTS / to Lieu^t Col^o JNO UPTON for ye said Land in / Joynture Ordered that ye said MARGARET UPTON / should be satisfied out of the s^d Lieu^t Col^o JOHN / UPTONs Estate Three Hundred and twenty / give pound Sterling. For accomplishment of / which payment as also towards the satisfying / of other Creditors to the said Estate the s^d MARGARET / was Impower'd to bring to Appraisement the Land / of the said L^t. Col^o JOHN UPTON by Order dated / at James City the 7th day of July 1653. and / to pay her self in the first place in Tobacco after / the Rate of Twenty Shillings ℔ Hundred wherein

[63]
she having proceeded and payed beyond Assetts and / obtained her Quietus est by two several Order at / James City bearing date ye 5th of October 1654 and / the 11th July 1655 Now this Indenture / Witnesseth that the said MARGARET UPTON / for the valuable Consideration of ffour Thousand five / Hundred Pounds of good Sound Virginia leaf / Tobacco & Cask to her already paid & delivered / by the said FRANCIS SLAUGHTER before ye Sealing & / Delivery hereof the Receipt whereof she doth / hereby acknowledge and to be fully satisfied / and contented there with hath Granted / Bargained & Sold and Confirmed and do by these / P^rsents fully clearly & absolutely Grant Bargain /

Sell & Confirm unto the s^d FFRRANCIS SLAUGHTER his / Heirs or Assigns for ever Eight Hundred & fifty / Acres of Land scituate lying & being in ye County / of the Isle of Wight upon the head of a Branch / proceeding out of Warrisqueak river now / known by the name of Newton Haven lying / N:N:W. upon the head of the said Branch and / running S:W. into the Woods and :E. upon the / said Branch which Branch doth near butt upon / the head of Pagan Point Creek the sd Land being / due to the said Lt Col^o JN^O UPTON by Patent under / the Seal of ye Colony dated ye 23^d of September / One Thousand six Hundred Thirty seven as by / the said Patent now at large may appear / part of which Land is now or lately in the / Tenure or Occupation of Capt JN^O ENGLISH. M^r. RICHARD / IZARD M^r. JOHN KING & M^r. LAWRENCE WARD, GYLES / LAWRENCE, THOMAS POOL & VINCENT BRADSHAW / To have and to Hold the said Eight / Hundred and fifty Acres of Land together with

[64]

all Teniments & immunities Priviledges Rights & / Profits as Also all Leases Counterparts of Leases / Grand-Patents and all other Records & Manuscripts / any ways relating or appertaining unto the said / Land or any part thereof to him the said / SLAUGHTER his Heirs & Assigns for ever And / the S^d MARGARET UPTON for her self Heirs Exec^{rs} / and Administrators do Covenant Promise and / Grant to and with the said FFRANCIS SLAUGHTER / his Heirs Exec^{rs} Adm^{rs}. & Assigns in manner & / form following (Viz) that at the Sealing & Delivery / hereof she hath good Right free and absolute / just & lawful title both in Law & Equity to / Bargain & Sell ye said Eight Hundred and / fifty Acres of Land & P^rmisses and every part / and parcel of them unto the said FFRANCIS / SLAUGHTER in manner & form aforesaid Holding / for good & lawful in Law for all Tennants upon / the said Land or any part thereof to turn / Tennants to the s^d FFRANCIS SLAUGHTER or his / assigns and do hereby as much as in her lye / and is valid make power of Livery of / Seizen of the said Eight Hundred & fifty Acres of / Land unto the said FFRANCIS SLAUGHTER with / power of Right to make Lease of Ejectment / or Ejectione ffirma for his better Title to the / P^rmisses or any part of them And do hereby / Covenant also to make further Assurance as by / good Council shall be devised advised and / required And Whereas there was a former / Grant of this Land made unto the said / SLAUGHTER bearing date July 5th: 1655 which / Grant was altogether Imperfect, Nevertheless

[65]

the Right of the said Land shall be in and to / the said SLAUGHTER from the Date of the former Grant / Witness my Hand & Seal the Day & Year above / written

Signed Sealed & Deliv^d   MARGARET **M:V.** UPTON

in Presence of Us
JN^O: BILLINGSLY. JN^O: ENGLISH:

    Capt. JOHN ENGLISH being Impowered by Letter / of Attorney under Hand & Seal from M^{rs}. MARGARET / UPTON did the 9° Augt 1656 in open Court / acknowledge this Deed according to Act and desired / it might be Recorded

    Teste. THO^S: WOODWARD ClCur

    Examined and truly Transcribed / Teste JA^S: BAKER ClCur

    To all to whom these Presents shall come I S^r / JOHN HARVEY K^t Governor and Captain General of Virginia / Now know Y^e that I the said S^r. JOHN HARVEY K^t. Do / with the Consent of the Council of State accordingly Give / and Grant unto PETER KNIGHT Merchant Two hundred Acres / of Land scituate lying & being in the County of the Isle of / Wight bounding upon ye main Creek S:E. Easterly and / South West or Westerly into the Woods butting upon ye Land / of Lieu^t JN^O UPTON Southerly and upon the Plantation / called by the name of the Batchelors Plantation North / erly the said Two Hundred Acres of Land being due / unto him the said PETER KNIGHT by Assignment and / Exchange by and with the said Lieu^t UPTON to and / with M^r. THOMAS HILL for Two Hundred Acres in / any other place Ungranted And by the said THOMAS

[66]
HILL being Conveyed Bargained & Sold to M^r. PETER / KNIGHT Merchant for a valuable Consideration To / Have and to Hold the said two Hundred / acres of Land &c Ut in Alijs: Given at / James City under my Hand and Sealed with the / Seal of the Colony this 13th of March 1638 &c
RICH^D: KEMP. Secretary   JOHN: HARVEY

    These Presents Witnesseth that I / PETER KNIGHT Merchant do Assigns all my Right & / Title of this Patent of Land unto JAMES INNES / or whom he may Assign it unto and do Promise / to save them harmless against any pretence of / Molestation of any Man Witness my Hand this / last of January 1655 in Virginia

                      ꝑ me PETER KNIGHT

Test ROBERT KEA:

M^r. ROBERT KEA:

Pray in my Behalf let ye Assignm^t of Land be / Acknowledged in Court as my Act and Deed / Witness my Hand this 26 January 1655

ℙ PETER KNIGHT

Recordatur 9: July. 1656

Exam^d & truly Transcribed / Teste JA^S: BAKER ClCur

[67]

Be it known unto all Men by these / presents that I SYLVESTER THATCHER of the County of Lancaster / Gent do for my self my Heirs & Assignes Sell Assign and / Set over and by these Presents Have Assigned Sold and / set over unto ANTHONY FFULGHAM all that part or parcel of / Land due unto me by Patent (wherein I did formerly / live) now in the Tenure and Occupation of RICHARD / WAY containing by Estimation One Hundred Acres / be it more or less scituate lying and being in the / County of the Isle of Wight bounded (viz) North / with Warrisqueak Bay West with the Creek South / with the Land now in ye Tennure of RICHARD MADDISON / NATHANIEL JONES & JOHN TOMLIN and with the Land / in the Tenure of THOMAS JONES formerly belonging / by Patent to Capt JOHN MOONs East with the Land / now in the Tenure & Occupation of the above named / ANTHONY FFULGHAM formerly granted by Patent to Mr. THOMAS DAVIS To have and to Hold / the said Land and every part & parcel thereof with / all Buildings Profitts Commodities Hereditaments / & Appurtenances Thereunto belonging & appertaining /to him the said FFULGHAM his Heirs Executors Adm^{rs} / and Assigns for ever without any Lett Claim Demand / Contradiction or Molestation of me my Heirs Executors / Administrators or Assigns or any other Person or Persons / whatsoever by my or their Consent Assent or Procurement / And I further bind my Self my Heirs &c to / deliver unto the said FFULGHAM his Heirs or Assigns the / Patent of the said Land with all my Right Title / and Interist therein and to put him in lawful / Possession of the said Land betwixt the Day of / this Date and the ffive & Twentieth day of December

[68]

next ensuing Witness my Hand & Seal this 16th: / day of December Anno Dom. 1654

Witness EDWARD SKYNNER   SYLVESTER S:T. THATCHER (Seal)
ROBERT: **R**: BIRD

Acknowledged and Delivered in the Isle of Wight / County Court by SILVESTER THATCHER the 9th July / 1656

Exam^d & truly Transcribed / Teste JA^S: BAKER ClCur

This Indenture made the 13th day of March / 1654 Between SAMUEL ELDRIDGE of the one part / and HUMPHRY CLARK of the other party Witnesseth / That the said SAMUEL ELDRIDGE hath clearly Bargained / and Sold and doth hereby clearly Bargain & Sell / unto the afore named HUMPHRY CLARK his Heirs Exec^{rs} / Adm^{rs} & Assigns for ever Two Hundred & Eighty Acres / of Land be it more or less being part of a Dividend of / land scituate on a Branch of the Blackwater taken up / and indented by the fores^d SAMUEL ELDRIDGE and / ROBERT FLAKE and divided (viz) the said Land as afore ment= / ioned / beginneth & boundeth on the Southside of ROBERT / FFLAKEs Land at a great standing Pine being at the Head / of a small forked reedy Branch and so down that Branch / to the Swamp and for Breadth of its half Miles runeth / upon the Barrens from the said Pine To have / Hold and peaceable Enjoy the said Land with all / priviledges Grants & Immunities whatsoever contained / and expressed in and by a Patent as more fully / may appear And the said SAMUEL ELDRIDGE for / himself his Heirs Exec^{rs} & Administrators doth

[69]

doth Warrant and hereby insure unto the said HUMPHRY / CLARK his Executors Administrators & Assigns a peaceable & / quiet possession of the P^{r}misses without the Eviction Expulsion / or Interruption of any Person or Persons by reason of any Title / or Claim formerly had or made to the same Acquitting & / discharging the said HUMPHRY CLARK his Heirs Executors &c / from all former Rents and Arrearages thereof The said / SAMUEL ELDRIDGE acknowledging hereby to have received full / Consideration & Satisfaction in and for the P^{r}misses In / Witness whereof and in Performance of all herein / contained the said SAMUEL ELDRIDGE hath hereunto put his / Hand & Seal the Day and Year above written
Signed Sealed and   SAMUEL **S** ELDRIDGE (Seal)
Deliv^d in P^{r}sence of
PETER BEDFORD   THOMAS **TW** WALTER

Recordatur 9th. July 1656

Examined & truly Transcribed / Teste JA^S: BAKER ClCur

Know all Men by these Presents that I JAMES / WATSON Tanner & MARY my Wife do for good & valuable / Consideration us thereunto moving already received Sell / Alienate & make over unto HENRY PITT his Heirs &

Assigns / for ever all our Right Title & Interist that we now have / or ever hereafter may have of two Hundred Acres of / Land being part of Mr JOHN SPARKES's Patent of / Seven Hundred & fifty Acres and Sold by the s^d / SPARKES Unto PETER HULL and after sold by the said HULL to / my Brother ROBERT WATSON and adjoyneth to the / Land of ANTHONY JONES where my Brother WATSON / formerly lived and now the said HENRY PITT / To have and to Hold the Premisses to

[70]
to him the said HENRY PITT his Heirs & Assigns for ever / with all Priviledges Liberties & Profits whatsoever / against any Persons whatsoever that may lay Claim / Challenge or Title to any part or parcel thereof either / from by or under us our Heirs Executors or Administrators / In Witness whereof we have hereunto affixed / our Hands & Seals this 10th day of March 1655

JAMES WATSON (Seal)

MARY **W** WATSON (Seal)

Acknowledged in the Isle of Wight County Court / the 12th of March 1655

Teste TH^O: WOODWARD Cl:Cur

Examined & truly Transcribed / Teste JA^S: BAKER ClCur

I HUMPHRY CLARK of the Isle of Wight County / Cooper being Sick & Weak in Body but of perfect / Memory do make & ordain this my last Will and / Testament in manner & form as followeth Impr^{is} / I do bequeath my Soul unto God expecting Mercy from / him in and through the Merits of Christ Jesus my only / Saviour & Redeemer and after my decease my Body / to be decently buried And for the rest of my / Worldly Estates after my Debts paid I do dispose / of in manner & form Following. I do Give unto / my Son JOHN CLARK and to his Heirs all Lands / whatsoever that do belong to me by any Rights / Patents or otherways whatsoever with the best / Feather-bed unto me now belonging with what / ffurniture belongs to it, with one half of what / Cattle are mine And the other Half I do Give / and Bequeath to my Wife, JANE CLARK. Item

[71]
I do Give more unto my loving Wife JANE CLARK / all my Household Stuff with all other my ffurniture / in the House as Linnen & Woolen only such excepted / as are in this my Will specified. Item I do / Give unto my Daughter in Law JANE BRUNT one / ffeather-Bed with what Furniture belongs to it / I do acknowledge that Six hundred pounds of Tobacco / due from JOHN SHERY

doth belong unto JANE BRUNT / Item I do give unto my two Kins Women JANE / HOW & MARY CLARK each of them one Cow Calf / to be delivered this Fall. And Whereas / MARY CLARK is a Covenant Servant for seven Years / I do remitt and give her Three Years of her Time / Item I do desire & appoint that my Servants / shall be kept togeather and the one half of / the Benefit of their Labour shall be made Use / of for the Maintenance of my Son JOHN CLARK / at School. Item I do Give unto THOMAS / HOLMES & JOHN WILLIAMS each of the one / Yearling Heifer. Item. I do Give unto W^M / GODWIN, JOHN WILLIAMS Welchman and my / Servant each of them one Cow Calf to be deliv^d / the next Fall after this. Item it is my Will / that my Wife JANE CLARK shall not make away / nor give at her decease any part of this Estate / from my Son JOHN CLARK but at her Decease / all which I have left to her for her Maintenance / to be properly his. Likewise I do make my / loving Wife JANE CLARK my lawful Executrix / and no other And I do Appoint my well / beloved ffriend ROBERT BIRD Overseer of this my / last Will for the performance of it to all true

[72]
Intents & purposes. Thus I do Renounce & Revoke / all former Wills nullifying them: and Ratifying / & Confirming this. In Witness whereof I have / hereunto set my Hand this 3° March: 1655
Witness THO^S HOLMES   HUMPHRY CLARK
W^M BRACEY
ALICE **C** BOSTOCK

Recordatur 9° Aprilis 1656

Exam^d & truly Transcribed / Teste. JA^S: BAKER ClCur

To all Christian People to whom / this present Writing shall come to be seen / I HENRY WATTS of the Isle of Wight County send Greeting / in our Lord God everlasting Whereas the Right / Honourable RICHARD BENNETT Esqr Governour and Captain / General of Virginia did by Letters Patents bearing date / the Six and Twentieth day of November 1652. Give / and Grant unto me the said HENRY WATTS four Hundred / fifty seven Acres of Land lying in the Isle of Wight / County af^d One Hundred fifty & seven Acres of the / said Land being formerly granted unto me the said / HENRY WATTS by Patent dated the 18th of October 1643 / and the other three Hundred Acres being also formerly / granted by Patent unto JOHN SPACKMAN dated the 13th / July 1635 and purchased of the said SPACKMAN by / me the said HENRY WEATTS which said ffour Hundred / fifty & seven Acres of Land is bounded as by the said / Letters Patent relation being thereunto had at large / appeareth. Now know Ye that I the said HENRY / WATTS for a valuable Consideration me hereunto moving

[73]

the Receipt whereof I hereby acknowledge Have Granted / Bargained Sole Alienated Assigned & set over And by / these P^{r}sents do Grant Bargain Sell Alien Assigns & set over / unto JOHN SYMPSON of the County af^d. His Heirs & Assigns / all that piece of parcel of Land now in the possession / of the said JOHN SYMPSON bounded by a little Creek / which parteth the said Parcel of Land and the Old ffeild / of me the said HENRY WATTS and so by the main Creek / to a marked Pine at the Oyster Bank and into the / Woods and so by marked Trees beyond the ffence of the / said JOHN SYMPSON which said parcel of Land is / part of the four Hundred fifty seven Acres by the said / Letters Patent granted as aforesaid To have / and to Hold the said parcel of Land hereby / granted unto the said JN^O SYMPSON his Heirs Executors / Adm^{rs} & Assigns for ever in as large & ample manner / to all Intents & Purposes as I my self may ought / or could hold ye same by vertue of ye s^d Letters Patent / together with all & singular Y^e Benefits Properties and / Profits thereof And I the said HENRY WATTS do / for my self my Heirs Executors / Administrators & Assigns shall & will Warrant and

[74]

Defend unto the said JOHN SYMPSON his Heirs Executors / Administrators & Assigns against all People for ever / by these Presents In Witness whereof I have / hereunto set my Hand & Seal this Nine & Twentieth / Day of December Anno Domini 1654
Signed & Delivered   HEN: WATTS. (Seal)
in the Presence of Us
RICH^D. SMITH W^M: WESTWRAY

    Accognitur in Curia Comitatus Insula / Vectis 16° Maij 1656 p HENRICUM WATTS / Recordatur 17° Maij 1656^8

    Examined & truly Transcribed / Teste JA^S: BAKER ClCur

    In the name of God Amen. / I ROBERT DUNSTER being Weak & sick of Body / but of sound & perfect Memory do bequeath my Soul / to God, my Sin to the Devil, and my Body to the / Earth to be buried in ye usual Burying Place.

---

    [8] "Acknowledged in the County Court of Isle of Wight the 16th of May by Henry Watts; recorded the 17th May 1656." This is a somewhat grander version of the earlier acknowledgement by the clerk.

And / for my Worldly Goods I dispose of it my this my / last Will & Testament as followeth. (viz) / Imprimis I give unto my dearly beloved Wife / all my Debts due to me either by Bill or Bond or / otherwise in Virginia. Item. I give unto my / beloved Wife likewise all my Cattle both Young & / Old Male & ffemale. Item. I give unto my / loving Wife all my Hoggs Male & Female. Item I give unto my loving Wife aforesaid

[75]

all my House-hold Goods whatsoever and all my wearing / Apparel and all my Books. Lastly. I give unto / my loving Wife this my now dwelling Plantation both / Housing & Ground. I give likewise unto my Brother / LEONARD DUNSTER half a Crown, and to his Son / WILLIAM DUNSTER half a Crown after my Decease / and all this to be fully Accomplished according to / The true Intent & Meaning hereof Witness my / Hand.

ROBERT: DUNSTER

Witness Us.
W^M: TRAVERS W^M JUX. ELIZABETH: **W**: WEBB & mark
THOMAS **T** WRIGHT
      Mark

      Recordatur 17° Maij 1656

      Examined and truly Transcribed / Teste JA^S: BAKER ClCur

      Articles of Agreement between / JOHN ASKUE of the one party and JOHN HAWKINS of the / other. Imprimis. It is agreed between the / above named Parties that the said JOHN ASKUE hath / sold unto JOHN HAWKINS the whole Plantation whereon / the said ASKEW now liveth with the Housing ffencing / and timber thereunto belonging also ffifty growing / Apple and all the Peach Trees & Cherry Trees now / standing on the said Plantation to be delivered unto y^e / said HAWKINS his Executors Adm^{rs} or Assigns to quietly enjoy / The said Land for ever from ye said ASKEW his Executors / Administrators or Assigns at or before the Twenty / fifth day of December next ensuing the date hereof / Item in Consideration the said HAWKINS is to pay

[76]

or cause to be paid unto the ASKUE ffive Thousand / Pound of Tobacco & Cask to be paid at two Payments / 2500 L^b Tob° in 1655 the other Payment in 1656 / Item the said ASKUE and his Wife is to acknowledge / The Sale of the said Land or Plantation in Court / unto the said HAWKINS or his Assignes for ever. / Item. The said ASKUE is to make Use of COOPERs / Timber to the Value of forty

Virginia Hogsheads / if in case the Timber be procured off the Head of / ye Land adjoining unto GEORGE ALLESON otherwise / the said ASKEW is to make Use of no more / Timber than the S^d ASKUE useth for his own Crop / Witness our Hands the Day & Year above written

JOHN ⚹ ASKUE

GEORGE ALLESON
Witness WILLM ⊢ PETTEFER   JOHN: HAWKINS

Recordatur 10°. Maij 1655

Examined & truly Transcribed / Teste. JA^S: BAKER ClCur

Be it known unto all Men by these Presents / that I JOHN NICHOLAS Planter at Corotoman River in / Rappahannock have Ordained & made and in my stead and / place by these P^rsents have Deputed put and Constituted / my trusty ffriend WILLIAM DENBIGH of Lancaster County / to be my true & lawful Attorney and in my Name / and to my Use to ask & demand of NICHOLAS GEORGE / Planter of the Isle of Wight County a full and true / just Assurance of the one half of a Patent of Seven / Hundred Acres of Land due & belonging unto me

[77]

the said NICHOLAS which half I have cause to be Seated / Giving and by these Presents Granting unto my said / Attorney full Power & lawfull Authority to ask and / demand of the said NICHOLAS GEORGE a firm Conveyance / for the same with Assignment from him and his Heirs / and also his Wife according to the Laws of the Country / and upon the Refusal & Denyal of the s^d Conveyance / my said Attorney having full Power by these P^rsents / to Use & Act such courses of Law as shall be requisite for / the Performance of the Premisses of the S^d NICHOLAS GEORGE / formerly to me the S^d JOHN NICHOLS in as large & ample / manner to all Intents & Purposes as if I were There & / psonally [--] In Witness whereof I have / hereunto set my Hand & Seal this 12° of May 1655
Sealed and Delivered   JN^O N NICHOLS (Seal)
In the Presence of
THO^S. T POWEL HOW POWEL

Recordatur 12°. Junij 1655

Examined & truly Transcribed / Teste JA^S: BAKER ClCur

We the Subscribers to this Verdict being impannelled as a Jury / by Order of the Isle of Wight Court dated the 9th June 1658 / in a difference betwixt

Major NICHOLAS HILL Pl[t] and JOHN / SNELLOCK Def[t] to see the Patent for Land which Major / HILL bought of Col° BERNARD wholly Surveyed. Have / in Obedience to the s[d] Order wth much Care & pain / observed the Surveyor to perfect & compleat the same / according to Patent to y[e] utmost of our Knowledge & / Judgments and do Testify that the Surveyor THOMAS

[78]

WOODWARD following the Head Line of the Mile upon / the Land on James River foremerly [sic] belonging to M[r]. JUSTINIAN COOPER came upon JOHN SNELLOCKs Land w[th]in / two Chains or thereabout of y[e] Northermost Branch of y[e] / Pagan Creek which parts The s[d] SNELLOCKs Land and / EDWARD PRINCE and so along the said Branch as / it runs upwards towards M[r]. CHARLES BARECROFTs to a / corner Tree of the said COOPERs and from thence / along y[e] Swamp to y[e] marked Trees of ELY and / PAWLIEs and to the Mill Dam and so down the / Swamp to y[e] head of Lawnes Creek and so along / The Land of ROBERT LAWRENCE to y[e] said LAWRENCEs / corner marked Tree joining upon COOPERs Line y[e] / Computation of the whole Patent of Col° BERNARD's / Land according to M[r]. THOMAS WOODWARDs Report / to Us being Nine Hundred Acres including therein / all the Housing & Land as aboves[d] that the / said JOHN SNELLOCK now lives upon which we do / find to belong to the said Major HILL according / to the Survey made by Us and M[r] WOODWARD / As Witness our Hands this 28th day of July 1658

THOMAS **T L**. LEWIS	THOMAS TABERER
S[T]. MOUNT: WELLS	ROBERT **R:B** BIRD
EDWARD **E:P**. PRYME	FRANCIS **F:I** INGLAND
PETER BEDFORD	CHARLES BARECROFT
THO[S] **T:C**: CHIVERS	EDMOND WICKINS
ROBERT: KEA	EDWARD BICKINOE

Examined & truly Transcribed / Teste JA[S]: BAKER ClCur

[79]

On the backside of a Conveyance for Land from AMBROSE / BENNETT to JOHN MOTLEY & THOMAS TURNER dated the 25th / day of June in the Twenty fifth Year of the Reign of King / Charles.[9] And Recorded in the Isle of Wight County the / 20th September 1643 [sic]. Which said

---

[9] The English had a tendency to count the first year of the Commonwealth as the 25th year of the reign of Charles I. This would technically be the year 27 Mar 1649-Mar 1650.

Conveyance was Assigned / by JOHN MOTELY & MARY his Wife to HENRY MOORES and / THOMAS TURNER the 17th April 1655 and recorded in y[e] / Isle of Wight County y[e] 10th March 1655. These Words / are Endorsed (viz) May: 10 1658. M[r]. ARTHUR / SKYNNER & WILLIAM ANDREWS Attorney of HENRY / MOORES on his Part and THOMAS TURNER for himself / did in Open Court make over all their Right unto / The Land and other particular mentioned in this / Conveyance unto M[r]. WILLIAM RUFFIN and his Heirs / or Assigns for ever

     Teste THO[S] WOODWARD ClCur

     Recordatur 10°: Maij 1658

Vide Original Conveyance   Exm[d] & truly Transcribed
     Folio. 21   Teste. JA[S]: BAKER ClCur

     In the name of God Amen. / I JOHN OLIVER being in good Health of Body and / bound for England do order & dispose of that Estate / the which it hath pleased God of his Mercy to / bestow upon me (in case it should please God to / take me to himself before I shall return hither to / Virginia again) as followeth. Imprimis / I Bequeath my Soul to God my Merciful Saviour / & Redeemer & my Body to be Buried and my

[80]
Debts being first paid. Item. I make my loving / Wife ELLIN OLIVER my full & whole Executrix of all / and every part of my Estate those Legacies hereafter / being first paid. For my Land on which I now live on / and Three hundred Acres of Land, which I have at / Blackwater I do Give & Bequeath unto my Two / Daughters equally between them. Item. I Give / and Bequeath unto my eldest Daughter Three Cows / out of my Stock of Cattle and their Increase / Item. I Give & Bequeath unto my Youngest / Daughter Three Yearling Heifers and Their Increase / and if any of these Cattle so given to my two Daughters / shall dye within this Year then my Will is that / Young Cattle shall be put in y[e] place & stead Thereof / out of y[e] remainder of my Cattle. Item. I Give / and Bequeath unto my two Daughters half a dozen of / Pewter Dishes to each of them Item. I Give & / Bequeath my Son JOHN a Cow Calf which is fatter this Year / Item for all the rest of my Estate I do leave it / wholly to my loving Wife whom before I have made / my whole Executrix to be at her disposing And / for the Performance of this my last Will and / Testament I do Appoint my loving friends, JAMES / PYLAND and ROBERT BIRD Overseers. In / Witness whereof I have hereunto set my / Hand & Seal this 19th of April. 1652
Testes JAMES PYLAND   JOHN: OLIVER (Seal)
JOHN BURTON

JOHN x REINING

Record[r]. 16: Junij 1655.

Examined & truly Transcribed / Teste JA[S]: BAKER ClCur

[81]

In the name of God. Amen. I / Captain JOHN MOON of the Isle of Wight County in Virginia / and Born at Berry near Gospert in y[e] Parish of Stoak / in Hampshire in England, being in Health and good / Memory (praised be God for it) do make this my last / Will & Testament in manner as followeth. O Lord / I have waited for thy Salvation, and now O Lord / into thy hands I commit my Soul or Spirit, for / Thou hast Redeemed it O Lord Thou God of Truth / and my Body unto y[e] Earth to be Interred in decent / manner being fully Assured of it's Resurection and / reuniting of it together again in that great Day / of God's Power. And all my Worldly Goods I / Give & Bequeath as in hereafter expressed.

Imprimis. I Give & Bequeath unto my loving & well / beloved Wife PRUDENCE MOON (my Debts being paid) one fourth / part of all my Movable Estate (that is to say) the same to be / equally divided between my Wife and my three Daughters / SARA, SUSANNA, & MARY MOON; and for my Land & Houses / I dispose of as followeth. I Give and Bequeath unto / my eldest Daughter SARAH MOON and to the Heirs of / her Body lawfully begotten for ever, my dwelling / House now named Bethlehem, with all y[e] Land & Houses / from Pagan Creek, and joining upon HENRY WATT's Land / unto y[e] Easterly side of the Reedy Swamp and to the / Mouth of y[e] Creek by the dwelling House. And unto / my second Daughter SUSANNA MOON I Give & Bequeath / all the Land & Houses from the Reedy Swamp to the / Westerly side of the Land that SAMUEL NICHOLS now / liveth upon, on the Easterly side of Bethlehem Creek / that Land now named Bethsaida to belong to her the / said SUSANNA and to the Heirs of her Body lawfully / begotten for ever. And to my Daughter MARY MOON / I Give & Bequeath all my Land & Houses y[t]. lyeth

[82]

on Red Point side now named Bethany with that which / DENNIS SYLLIVANT liveth upon and the Land belonging / to the Poplar Neck that lyeth by the King of all Places / all which to belong to the said MARY and to the heirs / of her Body lawfully begotten for ever. Now my Intent / and Will is that if my Daughter SARAH depart this / Life without Heir as aboves[d] that then Bethlehem her / Inheritance shall belong to my Daughter SUSANNA MOON / and her Heirs as aboves[d] for ever and that then half / Bethsaida which is my Daughter

SUSANNA's Inheritance / shall belong unto my Daughter MARY and her Heirs as / aboves[d] for ever and half SARAH's Moveables. Also / my Intent & Will is that is SUSANNA depart this Life / without Heir as aboves[d] before SARAH or MARY that / then her Inheritance belong wholly to MARY MOON and / her Heirs as aboves[d] for ever. As also if MARY depart / depart [sic] this Life without Heir as aboves[d] before SARAH or / SUSANNA MOON that then her Inheritance to belong wholly / unto SUSANNA MOON and her Heirs as aboves[d] for ever / And also if SARAH MOON and SUSANNAH MOON depart / this Life without Heirs as aboves[d] that then both their / Inheritances are to belong unto SARAH and her Heirs as / aboves[d] for ever and so accordingly and all other / things herein given & bequeathed my Intent & Will is / that it shall belong unto the Survivour of them and / her Heirs as aboves[d] accordingly for ever. And also / my Intent & Will is that my loving Wife PRUDENCE / MOON shall be in and abide & dwell in my / now dwelling House called Bethlehem House with / my Daughter SARAH MOON or SUSANNAH MOON or / MARY MOON or either Their Heirs for and during / The Widowhood of my well beloved Wife after / my Decease as also so much Land as in necessary / for her own particular Use for Planting & Pasture

[83]
during the Time aboves[d] And you my Children I charge / you all before God and the Lord Jesus Christ who / shall judge the Quick & the Dead that you demean / your selves loving, obedient, comfortable unto your Mother / all the days of her Life. And I Charge you my beloved / Wife that you provoke not your Children to Wrath / lest they be discouraged, but bring them up in the Nurture / & Admonition of the Lord; and live Peaceable & lovingly / together, and the God of Love & Peace will be with / You: and the Lord direct your ways in all things and / make you all to Increase & Abound in Love one towards / another and towards all Men and stablish your / Hearts unblamable in Holiness before God even our / ffather at y[e] coming of our Lord Jesus Xt with all his / Saints. And my Will is that my Brew House / and Land belonging to it at James Town be sold / toward y[e] Payment of my Debts. Also there is a / Certificate already granted for seven Hundred Acres / of Land and Rights for two Hundred more, which / Nine Hundred Acres of Land my Will is that it should / be taken up in some convenient place, and when it is / taken up; I Give and Bequeath three Hundred Acres / of it unto my Wife PRUDENCE MOON and her Heirs / for ever, and the other six Hundred Acres to be equally / divided between my three Daughters SARAH, SUSANNAH, / & MARY MOON, and their Heirs for ever in manner and / form as their other Inheritances afores[d] is expressed / Also I Give & Bequeath unto JOHN [sic] GARLAND my / Wives daughter four ffemale Cattle and two Hogsheads / of Tobacco to be delivered if she be living or to her Child /

if living the Year after my Decease. Also I give / and bequeath unto WILLIAM WILLSON my Wives Son / two ffemale Cattle and two Hogsheads of Tobacco

[84]

to be delivered if he be living the Year after my Decease / Also I give & bequeath unto PETER GARLAND My Wive's / Son in Law one Hogshead of Tobacco The Produce / whereof to be laid out in Plate and kept in / Rememberance of me, and if living the Tobacco to / be delivered as aboves[d]. And further for my Land / in England lying at Berry & Alverstoak in Hampshire / near Gosport & Portsmouth the which when I was / last in England I Mortgaged unto M[r]. OWEN JENNINGS / of Portsmouth for Two Hundred Pounds Sterling / Money my Will is that if you cannot redeem it / that then it be sold Outright and the Money to be / equally divided between my three Daughters SARAH / SUSANNAH & MARY MOON in manner as is aforesaid / only Ten Pounds Sterling of the Money that it is / sold for I give & bequeath unto the Poor of Berry / Five Pounds of it, and the other Five Pounds I / give unto y[e] poor of Alverstoak, which Money is to / be delivered into y[e] Hands of y[e] Overseers for the / Poor in each place to remain for a stock for y[e] Poor / to be lett out and the Interest thereof to be / given to the Poor in each Place yearly. Also there / is due to me Seven Pounds odd Money from M[r]. / JENNINGS which he being my Attorney received for / me for Rent due before y[e] Mortgage took place / and three Rundletts [sic] of Tobacco of about a / Hundred Pound weight that I left with him to / sell for my Use but I have not received any thing / from him since this also to be divided as aboves[d] / Also I give and bequeath four ffemale Cattle / to remain for a Stock for ever for Poor Fatherless / Children that hath nothing left them to bring them

[85]

up, and for Old People past their Labour, or Lame / People that are destitute in this Lower Parish of / the Isle of Wight County: the ffemale from time to / time to de [sic] disposed to those that do keep such persons / to have the Milk, Provided that those that have / them be careful of those they receive and of their / Increase; My Will is that all y[e] ffemale Increase / from time to time be & remain for a Stock for / this Use, and the Male Cattle & old Cows to be / disposed of for Cloathing & Schooling and the like / necessaries for such Persons in Condition as is before / expressed, and the Overseers of the Poor with Consent of / my Children from time to time are to see this my / Will in this particular frealy performed as it is in my Will expressed and not / otherways

Recordatur 12° Augusti 1655

Examined & truly Transcribed / Tests. JA[S]: BAKER ClCur

These Presents Testify that we JOHN / DRUETT and MARGARET Wife of the said JOHN who was / formerly the Widdow or Relict of RICHARD WILLIAMSON / deceased and Adm^x of his Estate do for us our Heirs / Executors & Administrators upon a valuable Consideration / in hand given wherewith we are fully satisfied Sell / Bargain & Alienate unto THOMAS ELMES his Heirs Executors / Administrators & Assigns for ever all that parcel of Land / Conveyed to the said MARGARET by GEORGE BROWN & / ELIZABETH his Wife by Bill of Sale dated the Twenty / first of September 1655. scituated at the Norther side / of the Indian ffeild in the Upper Parish of the Isle

[86]

of Wight County containing three Outs or Sixty Pole square / joining to the marked Trees at ye Mile end of Land / some time belonging to RICHARD BENNETT Esqr To / Have and to Hold the said Land with all / Priviledges Royalties Profits or Emoluments w^{t}soever / to him y^e said THOMAS ELMES his Heirs Executors / Administrators & Assigns with General Warranty / against all Persons And further we the said / JOHN DRUETT & MARGARET / do Assign all our / Right Title & Interist to all the Marsh ad= / joining to the said Indian ffield which we / have or any ways Claim by Vertue of an / Order of the Governor & Council dated the / 24th / March 1654 unto the said THO^S. ELMES / his Heirs Executors Administrators & Assigns / for ever Acknowledging hereby that we are fully / satisfied for the same. In Witness whereof / we have hereunto set our Hands & Seals / this 2^d Day of August Anno Domin: One Thousand Six / Hundred fifty and Nine

Signed Sealed and   JOHN **T** DRUETT   (Seal)
D^d in ye P^{r}sences of Us   MARGARET DRUETT
WILL^M **WD** DAWSON
WILLIAM LEWER.

JOHN DRUETT & his Wife MARGARET acknowledged / this as their Act & deed at a Court held

[87]

in the Isle of Wight County the 9° Augt 1659

Teste THO^S: WOODWARD ClCur

Examined and truly Transcribed / Teste. JA^S: BAKER ClCur

Be it known unto all Men by / these Presents that I THOMAS HINSON do acknowledge to / have sold unto WILLIAM BRUNT a parcel of Land upon / the South side of ye ffence of JOHN NEWTON running / up to ye White marsh by a great Swamp the Land / lying between One Hundred Acres of JAMES WATSON / And that the said WILLIAM BRUNT is to have it for / ever with as good Assurance as the said JOHN SEWARD / hath given me the said THOMAS HINSON by his Patent / And Furthermore if in Case the said WILLIAM / BRUNT doth Lease the said Land and that Mr. RICHARD / PITT do require it I THOMAS HINSON do bind him Self / to pay One thousand Weight of Tobacco & Cask / unto ye said WILLIAM BRUNT. Witness my Hand / this first day of December 1643

Witness JOHN NEWTON   THOMAS: HINSON

Know all Men by these presents that I WILLIAM / BRUNT do hereby Assign & Consign all my Right & / Title of this parcel of Land unto THOMAS KEERKE / according to the Tenure of this Patent Witness / my Hand This 19th of October 1644

JOHN NEWTON   WILLIAM x BRUNT

Vide further Assignm^t over Leaf

[88]

Know all Men by these Presents that I THOMAS / KEERKE do Assigns and turn over unto NICHOLAS / ALDRED all my Right & Interist of this Parcel of / Land according to the full Intent of this Bill / Witness my Hand this 23^d of November 1645

Test ROB^T. WATSON   THOMAS KEERKE

Know all Men by these Presents that I / NICHOLAS ALDRED do Assign & turn over unto / PHILIP PARRY all my Right & Interist of this / parcel of Land according to ye Sense of this Patent / as Witness my Hand

Recordatur 10 September 1655

Examined & truly Transcribed. / Teste JA^S: BAKER ClCur

Know all Men by these Presents that I / Major GEORGE FAWDON do for my Self my Heirs and / Assigns freely Give unto ISAAC GEORGE the Son of / Major JOHN GEORGE One Hundred Acres of Land next / adjoining to the Land of the said Major JOHN GEORGE on / the Upper side to him the said

ISAAC and his Heirs for / ever Provided that he liveth to the Age of One and / Twenty. But in the mean time I the said Major / FFAWDON do enjoyn my Self to give the said ISAAC present / Possession and to give him Conveyance for ye said Land / to the said Purpose at the next County Court in the / Isle of Wight County. Further it is Agreed that if in

[89]
Case the said ISAAC GEORGE shall decease before the Age of / One & twenty Years then the said Land to return to / the said Major FAWDON   Witnes my Hand this / 27 of October 1654

GEORGE FAWDON

J: BARCLY
TANTEMOUNT[10] WELLS

      Endorsed thus.

      Memorandum that I NATHANIEL BACON / Administrator of the Estate of Major GEORGE FFAWDON in / the Behalf of M^rs. ANN FAWDON the Relict of the said / FFAWDON do in all Points Confirm unto ISAAC GEORGE / Son of M^r. JOHN GEORGE the full Contents of this / Gift of Land within written And do enjoyn my / Self as Administrator upon Demand to give Sufficient / Conveyance for the same unto the said M^r. GEORGE on the / Behalf of his Son Witness my Hand this 9° July / 1655

NATHANIEL BACON

      Recordatur 12 Augustij 1655

      Examined and truly Transcribed / Teste JA^S: BAKER ClCur

[90]
      Know all Men by these Presents that I / CHRISTOPHER LEWIS have Sold & delivered unto JOHN / GUTTERIDGE one Parcel of Land unto him the afores^d / JOHN GUTTERIDGE or his Executors Adm^rs & assigns for / ever the Land bordering upon FFRANCIS ENGLAND and / lying upon the East side of the Swamp this Land / I the said CHRISTOPHER LEWIS do Confirm unto JN^O / GUTTERIDGE all the Land that the said LEWIS holds by / Patent of the Eastward side of the said Swamp only / one parcel of Land that is called by the name of the / ffork of ye Branch this Land I the said LEWIS do / Confirm unto

---

    [10] This name should be "St. Mount," but the scribe may be having a small joke at the witness's expense.

the said GUTTERIDGE or his Assigns for / ever free from the Disturbance of me the s^d XTOPHER / LEWIS Witness my Hand this 5th of December 1651

Signed and Delivered   CHRISTOPHER: **C** LEWIS

In the Presence of   mark

RICHARD EGLESTON JAMES JAKINS

Acknowledged by the s^d LEWIS in Court / Recordatur March 10 1654

Examined and truly Transcribed / Teste JA^S: BAKER ClCur

To all People to whom this present Writing / shall come I CHARLES BARCROFT send Greeting in the / Lord God Everlasting. Know Ye that I the said CHARLES / BARCROFT as well for and in Consideration of ye natural / Affection & Love which I have & do bear unto my / well beloved Wife MAGDALIN BARECROFT and my Son

[91]

BARCROFT as also for divers other good Causes & / Considerations me at this present especially moving / Have Given and Granted and by these Presents do / Give Grant and Confirm unto ye s^d MAGDALIN BARCROFT / and WILLIAM BARCROFT all and singular my Goods / Chattels Hoggs Plantation Servants Pewter Brass / Household Stuff Apparel Beding Bills Bonds and / all other my Substance whatsoever Movable & Immovable / Quick & Dead of kind nature of quality or condition / whatsoever the same are to be and in what Place or / places so ever the same be shall or may be found / well in my own Custody or Possession as in the Possession / Hands Power or Custody of any other Person or Persons / whatsoever. To Have and to Hold all / and singular ye said Goods Chattels Hoggs Debts and / all other ye afores^d Prmisses unto the s^d MAGDALIN / BARECROFT & WILLIAM BARECROFT to their own proper Use / and Behoof for ever freely & quietly without any / Matter of Challenge Claim or Demand of me the said / CHARLES BARCROFT or of any other Person or Persons w^{t}soever / for me in my Name by my Cause Means or Procurement / and without any Money or other thing therefore to be / yielded paid or done unto me the said CHARLES BARCROFT / my Executors or Assigns and I the said CHARLES BARCROFT / all and singular the said Goods Chattels Hoggs Debts and / Premisses to the said MAGDALEN BARCROFT & W^M: BARECROFT / their Executors or assigns against all People do Warrant / and do ever defend by these Presents And further / know Ye that I the said CHARLES BARECROFT have / put the said MAGDALEN BARECROFT & WILLIAM BARECROFT / in Peaceable & quiet Possession of all & singular / the afores^d Premisses by the delivery unto them at

[92]

the ensealing hereof One coyned Piece of Sylver commonly / called Two pence fixed on the Seal of these Presents / In Witness whereof I the aforesaic CHARLES BARECROFT / have hereunto set my Hand & Seal this 10th day of / April 1654

Sealed & Delivered   CHARLES: BARCROFT. (Seal)
In ye Presence of
RICHARD WILLIAMS GEORGE MOOR

A piece of Two-pence Pendant

Recordatur 12: Martij 1654

Examined and truly Transcribed / Teste JA^S: BAKER ClCur

To all Christian People to whom / these presents shall come I GEORGE FAWDON of the / Isle of Wight County send Greeting in our Lord God . Everlasting To whom be it known that I the / said GEORGE do Give & Gran and by this my / Present Writing do Assigns unto M^{rs}. ANN SMITH / whom : intend to make my Wife ffifteen Hundred / Acres of Land lying in the Uppe Parish of the / af^d Isle of Wight County upon the Main River / side beginning a JOB BEAZLIEs Plantation joining / to the Land that was formerly JOHN OLIVERS at / a Mulberry Tree marked upon ye Sands and / running up the saic River to ye Land of RICHARD / CORSEY and backward into the Woods unti the / said ffifteen Hundred Acres of Land shall be/ Completed To have and tc hold

[93]

the said Land to her her Heirs & Assigns for ever after my / Death. Also I Give and Assign unto her upon ye same / Consideration & Condition six Cowes anc two Mares. In / Witness whereof I have hereunto set my Hand & Seal / this 30^t day of October 1654

Witness   GEORGE: FAWDON (Seal)
RICH^D: CLARK. THO^S: WOODWARD

Att which above mentioned Jointure & Dowry the Nuptials / being now Celebrated We GEORGE & ANN FFAWDON do / Oblidge our Selves never tc Alienate Release or in any / ways alter without the Consent & Approbation of ou / Father in Law NATHANIEL BACON and our Mother ANN his / Wife with ou Brother WILLIAM SMITH

Witness   GEORGE FAWDON

THO^S: WOODWARD RICHARD CLARK   ANN FAWDON

Recordatur 16 Martj 1654

Examined & truly Transcribed / Teste JA^S: BAKER ClCur

All Men shall know by these Presents that I GEORGE / LOBB for the valuable Consideration of ffourteen Hundred / Pounds of Tobacco & Cask by me already received / have Alienated Bargained & Sold and do by these / Presents for my self my Heirs Executors Adm^rs & Assigns / by Vertue of a Letter of Attorney from Capt. JAMES CRANIDGE / & ALICE his Wife to me directed Alienate Bargain & / Sell unto RICHARD JORDAN his Heirs Exec^rs Adm^rs & Assigns / to say ffifty Acres of Land lying upon the Long Pond / Creek once in the possession of HUGH LEE and after pur= / chased by WILLIAM CRANIDGE deceased all which s^d Land

[94]

of ffifty Acres as afores^d with the Benefitts & Profits to / the same belonging I the said GEORGE LOBB do Warrant / to save defend & keep harmless the said RICHARD JORDAN / his Heirs Executors Adm^rs or Assigns from any Person or / Persons w^tsoever laying Claim thereunto To Have Hold / Occupy Possess and quietly enjoy the said ffifty / Acres of Land with all the Rights Priviledges and / Immunities thereunto belonging to him he said RICHARD / JORDAN his Heirs & Assigns for ever. In Witness / whereof I the said GEORGE LOBB have hereunto set / my Hand & Seal this 21 day of December Anno / Domini 1653
Signed Sealed and Delid^d   GEORGE LOBB (Seal)
in the Presence of
RICHARD SHARP ANTHONY **A** MATHEWS

Examined & truly Transcribed / Teste JA^S: BAKER ClCur

This Indenture made the five and twentieth / Day of April in the One and twentieth Year of the Reign of / of [*sic*] our Sovereign Lord Charles by the Grace of God of / Ingland Scotland France and Ireland King Defender / of the Faith &c. Between JUSTINIAN COOPER of the / Isle of Wight County in Virginia Gent and ANNE his / Wife of the one Party and JOHN GEORGE of the same Place / Gent. Of the other Part Witnesseth that We the said / JUSTINIAN COOPER and ANNE my Wife for and in / Consideration of two Stears of the Age of five Years to / us

[95]

us in Hand already paid by the s^d. JOHN GEORGE before the / Ensealing and Delivery of these Presents of and from / which payment we do fully discharge him his Heirs / Executors & Adm^{rs}: and also for and in Consideration of / the Sum of fifteen Hundred Pounds of Tob^o: to be paid / unto us at the next Crop insueing and other especial / Consideration us hereunto moving have Given Granted / Bargained Sold Aliened assigned and set unto and by / these Presents doth Give Grant Bargain sell, alien / assigne and set over unto the s^d. JOHN GEORGE his Heirs / and Assigns forever all that two whole Parcels / of Land adjoining together in the Isle of Wight County / commonly called by the Name of ROBERT BENNETs and the / Quarter Land containing by Estimation two Hundred / Acres be it more or less being Part of a Patent of two / Thousand four Hundred Acres Dated the 16th Day of / March 1642 Granted unto the s^d. JUSTINIAN COOPER / which s^d: two Hundred Acres of Land be it more or less / Bounded as followeth (Viz^t:) East upon the main / River Westerly unto the Woods South upon the Cypress / Swamp and North upon the marked Trees of a Parcell / of Land now in the Tenure of FRANCIS PLAISE together / with all Houses outhouses Edifices Buildings Orchards / Gardens and all other Appertinances & Previledges / thereunto belonging or in any Wise appertaining / To have & to hold the s^d: two Hundred Acres of Land / be it more or less Houses and other the forementioned / Premises bounded as afores^d: with his due Share of / all Mines and Minerals therein contained, and with / all Rights and Previledges thereunto belonging / unto the s^d: JOHN GEORGE, his Heirs, and Assigns forever / in as ample Manner to all Intents & Purposes / as

[96]

as the s^d: Premises are or have been formerly Granted to him / the s^d: JUSTINIAN COOPER or ANNE is Wife either by Patent / or any other Conveyance his Heirs or Assigns To have / & to hold the said forerecited Premises and evry Part and / parcel thereof, under the Tenures Rents Services and / Conditions in any of the s^d: Deeds of Grant mentioned / and expressed unto the s^d: JOHN GEORGE his Heirs & Assigns / forever And the s^d: JUSTINIAN COOPER and ANNE his Wife / for themselves their Heirs Executors Adm^{rs}: & assigns doth / Covenant to and with the s^d: JOHN GEORGE his Executors / Adm^{rs}: or assigns that he is at this present seised of an / indefeazable Estate in the Premises in Fee simple according / to the Tenure & Purport of the forementioned Deed of Grant / and that the said Premises are free and clear and shall / be always made free and clear by the s^d: JUSTINIAN COOPER / & ANNE his Wife, their Heirs, Executors Admrs: & Assigns / from all former Grants, Bargains, Sales Jointers / Dowers, Judgments, Executions, or any other Incumbrance / had, made, done or suffered by the s^d: JUSTINIAN COOPER & ANNE / his Wife and the said JUSTINIAN COOPER & ANNE his Wife / doth by these Presents further Covenant and Grant to and / with the s^d: JOHN GEORGE his Heirs and Assigns,

that he the / s^d^: JUSTINIAN COOPER his Heirs, Executors, and Adm^rs^: shall / and will at all Times hereafter, Warrant and Defend the / forementioned premises to the s^d^: JOHN GEORGE his Heirs / and Assigns against him the s^d^: JUSTINIAN COOPER and / ANNE his Wife, their Heirs, and Assigns, against any / other Person or Persons whatsoever claiming from by / or under them the s^d^: JUSTINIAN COOPER and ANNE his Wife / In Witness whereof the parties to these Presents have / interchangeably put to their Hands & Seals the Day & Year / first above Written
Ex^d^ & Truly Transcribed
Test JA^S^. BAKER ClC^r^   JUSTINIAN COOPER (Seal)
Witness GEORGE FAUDON   ANNA COOPER (Seal)
the Mark of **T C** THO^S^: CARTER

[97]
       This Indenture made the fifteenth Day of April / in the Year of our Lord God One Thousand six Hundred forty and / six Between EDWARD PRINCE of the one Part and GEORGE / STEPHENS GEORGE HARDY and JOHN WATKINS of the other / Part Witnessith That the s^d^: EDWARD PRINCE for the valuable / Consideration of seventeen Thousand five Hundred / Pound Weight of Virginia Tobacco hath and by these Presents / Doth Demise Give Grant Bargain alienate and forever / Assign and make over unto the s^d^: GEORGE STEPHENS GEORGE / HARDY and JOHN WATKINS their Heirs Executors Adm^rs^ / & Assigns One Water Mill sicuate lying and being at / the Head of Lawns Creek in the County of Isle of Wight / with all Housing Land Erections Works whatsoever / with all and ev'ry Thing properly belonging & appertain / ing to the s^d^: Mill, with all Previldeges Rites and / Preheminences whatsoever. To have & to hold / the s^d^: Mill with all Titles & Previledges belonging / thereto, and with Warranty by him the s^d^: PRINCE his Heirs / Executors Adm^rs^: &c. to them the s^d^: STEPHENS HARDY and / WATKINS, their Heirs Executors Adm^rs^: &c Assigns forever / from him the s^d^: PRINCE his Heirs &c. and from all Manner / of Person & Persons whatsoever In Witness whereof / I / the s^d^: EDWARD PRINCE hath hereunto set his Hand and / Seal the Day & Year first above Written
Signed Sealed & delivered and
Possession Given of the Mill   EDWARD PRINCE
By Delivery of the Key of the Mill   the Seal
House being part for the whole
in presence of us
JOHN HAMMOND JAMES BREWER
STEPHEN WEBB

      Examined & Truly Transcribed Test JA^S^: BAKER ClCur

[98]

This Indenture made the five and twentieth Day of / June Anno Dom 1644 Between ROBERT ELEY of the one Part / and WILLIAM TROLODER of the other Part. Witnesseth, That I / the s^d: ROBERT ELEY for me my Heirs, Executors, Admo^rs: and / Assigns, do Ratifie, avouch, Convey, and forever confirm unto / the said WILLIAM TROLODER his Heirs, Executors Admo^rs: and / Assigns One Hundred and fifty Acres of Land which I the / s^d: ROBERT ELEY took up for him the s^d: WILLIAM TROLODER for / the Transportation of three Servants, into this Colony / which said one Hundred and fifty Acres of Land is / situate lying and being in the Isle of Wight County being / the Southerly & outermost Bounds of his the s^d: ROBERT / ELEYs Patent To have & to hold all and singular / the s^d: One Hundred and fifty Acres of Land with his due / Share of all Mines and Minerals therein contained and / with all rights Privildeges [--] and Commodities / thereunto belonging or in any ways appertaining unto him / the s^d: WILLIAM TROLODER his Heirs Executors, adm^rs: and Assigns / forever in as clear and ample Manner to all Intents and / Purposes as is expressed in a Charter of Orders from the late / Treasurer and Company bearing Date the 18th: of November 1618 / as in and by the s^d: ROBERT ELEYs Patent more at large appear / bearing date at James Citty the 17th: day of September Anno / Domini 1639 &c To be held of our Sovreign Lord the King / his Heirs and Successors as of his Mannour of East / Greenwich in free and common Soccage and not in Capite / nor by Knights Service Yeilding and paying unto our / s^d: Sovreign Lord the King or to his Rent=gatherers for the s^d: / One Hundred and fifty Acres of Land, three shillings Sterling / Yearly to his Majesty at the Feast S^t: Michael the Arch / Angel as in and by his the s^d: ROBERT ELEYs patent / Whereunto

[99]

Relation being had more at large it doth and may appear / In Witness whereof, I the s^d: ROBERT ELEY have hereunto set my / Hand & Seal interchangeably the Day and Year above mentioned
Sealed Signed & Delivered
in the Presence of us   ROBERT ELEY (Seal)
WILLIAM WHITAKER
WILLIAM WARINGE

Examined & truly Transcribed / Teste JA^S: BAKER Cl Cur

These Presents Witness That I WILLIAM TROLODER do / assigne over all my Right and Title of this Conveyance of / One Hundred and fifty Acres of

Land out of ROBERT ELEY's / Patent unto THOMAS WATTON or his Assigns forever to / injoy. Witness my Hand this 11th: of January 1645
HENRY JOHNSON   his
ARTHUR **W** WOOD his mark   WILLIAM **WT** TROLODER
                                                                                    Mark

Examined & truly Transcribed / Test JA^S: BAKER Cl Cur

To all to whom This present Writeing shall come / to be seen I ANTHONY JONES of the Isle of Wight County in / Virginia Gen^t. Send Greeting. Know ye That I the s^d: ANTHONY / JONES for and in Consideration of the Sum of seven / Hundred Pounds of good Merchantable Tobacco to me in / Hand paid before the ensealing hereof by ROBERT WINCHELL and / WILLIAM SMARLEY of the same County Planters whereof I do / acknoledge the Receipt by the Presents Have Bargained / & Sold and by these Presents do fully & absolutely / Bargain and sell unto the s^d: ROBERT and WILLIAM their / Heirs

[100]
Heirs & Assigns forever one Parcel of Land adjoining to the / land of me the s^d: ANTHONY on the East Side, And one other / the Lands there of WILLIAM LEWIS on the North Side as the / same is bounded by marked Trees, the Bredth thereof lyeth / between the Fleskett [*sic*, "freshet"] Swamp on the West Side, and one other / Swamp called the Deep Swamp on the East Side together / with all the Estate, Right, Title, and Interest that I have / or may claim for to have of in or to the s^d: Land, or any / Part thereof To have & to hold the s^d: Land & ev^ry / Parcel thereof unto the the [*sic*] s^d: ROBERT and WILLIAM or either / of them their Heirs & Assigns to the proper Use and / Behoof of the s^d: ROBERT WINCHELL and WILLIAM SMARLEY / their Heirs and Assigns forever with general Warrantee / against all People In Witness whereof I the s^d: ANTHONY / JONES have hereunto set my Hand and Seal dated the / 25th Day of March Anno Dom 1639 And in the fourteenth / Year of the Reign of our Sovreign Lord King Charles of / Ingland &c.
Signed Sealed & Delivered
in the Presence of   ANTH^O: JONES (Seal)
JOHN GYLES
RICHARD JORDAN
        Examined & truly transcribed.

        Be it Known unto all Men by these Presents / that I FARRAR FLINTON of the Isle of Wight County in Virginia / Chirurgeon for and in Consideration of the Sum of one Thousand / fifty and four Pounds of good Merchantable Tobacco, in Leaf to / be in Hand paid by JOHN SNELLOCK of the County afores^d. / Planter whereof I do acknoledge the Receipt and therewith / myself fully satisfied and contented by these Presents have / Bargained

[101]
Bargained and Sold and do hereby fully and absolutely / Bargain and Sell unto the s^d: JOHN SNELLOCK all my Plantation / where I now live containing One Hundred and fifty Acres / with the Houses thereupon erected and standing with all the / Rights Members and Appirtinances to the same belonging / To have and to hold the same and every Part thereof / unto the s^d: JOHN SNELLOCK his Heirs Executors and Assigns / to their own proper Use forever Provided always and upon / Condition notwithstanding that if I the s^d: FARRAR FLINTON / my Heirs Executors and Adm^rs: or any of us do truly pay / or cause to be paid unto the s^d: JOHN SNELLOCK his Executors / Adm^rs: or Assigns the s^d: Sum of One Thousand fifty & four / Pounds of Tob° and one sufficient Hogshead, on or before the / last day of January now next comeing That then this present / Writing and the Sale of the Premises hereby made shall be/ utterly void and of none Effect In Witness whereof I have / hereunto set my Hand this 18th: of April 1646
Signed and Delivered
In the Presence of   FARRAR FLINTON
R^I: W^M:SON JOHN NEWMAN

Examined and truly Transcribed / Test JA^S BAKER ClCur

This Indenture made the 19th: day of October in the / fourth Year of the Reign of our Sovreign Lord Charles by the Grace / of God of Ingland, Scotland, France and Ireland King Defender of / the Faith &c Between GYLES JONES of Elizabeth City Gent / of the one Part and JUSTINIAN COOPER of Warwicksqueak Gent / and ANNE his now Wife late the Widow and Relict of JAMES HARRIS [11] / Planter

---

[11] James Harris was in reality James Harrison, as indicated by the following reference: H. R. McIlwaine, ed., *Minutes of the Council and General Court of Colonial Virginia*, 2nd ed. (Virginia State Library: Richmond, VA, 1979), p. 35. "laste day of November 1624…Whereas Capt. [RAPHE] HAMER Compleyned in Courte for ye recovery of A Dept of 250 pownd waight of Tobacco, due to be paide by Ensigne JAMES HARRISON deceased and DAVID BARRY and JOHN COSTARDE, likewise Deceased, as Ptners together for as much as noe prooffe was made of their Ptner ship and for y^t did appeare by two servants that were only left alive, That they did Pply belong to the saide JAMES HARISONE, as by the deposition of the said servants appeareth, y^t is

[102]

Planter deceased of the other Part Witnesseth That the said / GYLES JONES for divers good and valuable Considerations him / thereunto espeacially moving and also for and in Consideration / of the Sum of 1230 Pounds Weight of Good and Merchantable / Tob°: to him in Hand paid at or before the ensealing hereof by the / s^d JUSTINIAN COOPER whereof and wherewith he doth acknoledge / himself fully satisfied and paid and thereof and of every Part / thereof doth acquit and discharge the s^d: JUSTINIAN COOPER forever / by these Presents Hath Given Granted Bargained Sold / Aliened Enfeoffed and Confirmed and by these Presents Doth / Give Grant Bargain Sell Alien Enfeoff and Confirm unto the / s^d. JUSTINIAN COOPER and ANNE his s^d: Wife and their Heirs and / Assigns for One Hundred Acres of Land lying & being in / the Bottom of Warwicksqueak Bay abutting North upon the / late Mansion House of the s^d. GYLES JONES, South upon the Main / Land and East and West upon the Great River which s^d: One / Hundred Acres of Land were amongst other Things by Patent / Dated the 14th Day of December 1619 Given and Granted by / S^r. GEORGE HARVY K^t: then Governour and Captain Generale / of Virginia unto the s^d. GYLES JONES his Heirs & Assignes forever / As by the s^d: Patent whereunto Refference being had more / fully doth and may appear And all and singular Houses / Edifices and Buildings thereupon erected and built with / all Rights Priviledges and Appertinances to the same / Premises of any Part thereof belonging or appertaining / To have & to hold the said one Hundred Acres of Land / and all and Singular other the before Bargained Premises / afores^d. and every Part and Parcel thereof with their and ev^{r}y of / their appertinances unto the said JUSTINIAN COOPER and ANNE / his Wife their Heirs and Assigns forever To the only proper / Use and Behoof of them the said JUSTINIAN and ANNE / their Heirs and assigns forever Yielding and paying therefore / yearly

[103]

Yearly unto the Rent gatherers appointed for the publick Uses / at the Feast of S^t: Michael the Archangel the fee Rent of two / Shillings. And the said GYLES JONES the s^d: One Hundred Acres of / Land, and all and Singular other the Premises afores^d: and / ev^{r}y Part and Parcel thereof with the Appertinances / whatsoever, unto them the s^d: JUSTINIAN COOPER and ANNE / his Wife and their Heirs, against him the said GYLES JONES / & his Heirs, shall and will forever hereafter, warrant and / Defend and harmless keep. In Witness whereof the Partys / first above named, to this Present Indenture interchangeably / have put their Hands and Seals the Day & Year first / above written

---

therefore ordered y^t ANNA COOPER late wiefe to the said JAMES HARISONE, doe onely Satisfie the Pper debts dew by the said JAMES HARRISONE."

69

Sealed & Delivered in   GYLES JONES
the presence of
JOSEPH PAIGE WESSELL WEBLING}

      Examined & truly transcribed

       This Indenture made the 29th day of September / Anno Dom 1629 and in
the fifth Year of the Reign of our / Sovreign Lord King Charles by the Grace of
God of Ingland / Scotland, Frances and Ireland Defender of the Faith &c
Between / JUSTINIAN COOPER of Warwicksqueak Gent and ANNE his now
Wife, late the Widdow and Relict of JAMES HARRIS Planter deceased / of the
one Part and WASSALL WEBLIN and GEORGE FADOINE of Warwicksqueak
/ afores[d]. Planter of the other Part Witnesseth That the said / JUSTINIAN
COOPER as well for divers good Causes & Considerations / him thereunto
especially moving as also for and in Consideration / of the Sum of Seven
Thousand Pounds Weight of good merchantable / Tobacco, Five Thousand
Pounds thereof, to him the s[d]. JUSTINIAN / COOPER

[104]
COOPER in Hand Paid before the insealing hereof by the said / WASSELL
WEBLIN and GEORGE FADOINE the Receipt thereof, the said / JUSTINIAN
COOPER doth hereby acknoledge, and thereof ev'ry Part / and Parcel thereof
doth acquit and discharge the said WASSELL / WEBLIN and GEORGE
FADOINE, remaining due unto the said / JUSTINIAN 2000 pounds Weight by
Specialty Hath Given / Granted Bargained Sold Aliened Infeofed and Confirmed
and / by these presents Doth Give Grant Bargain Sell Alien Infeof and / Confirm
unto the s[d]. WEBLIN and GEORGE FADOINE and their Heirs / and Assigns
forever One Hundred acres of Land lying and / being in the Bottom of
Warwicksqueak Bay abutting North / upon the late Mansion House of GILES
JONES Planter / South upon the main Land and East and West upon the / Great
River which said one Hundred Acres of Land were / amongst other Things by
Patent dated the fourteenth day / of December One Thousand six Hundred and
Nineteen Given / and Granted by S[d]. GEORGE [--] Knight then Governer / and
Captain General of Virginia unto GILES JONES his / Heirs and Assigns forever
as by the said Patent whereunto / Reference being had more fully doth and may
Appear / And all and Singular Houses Edefices and Buildings / thereupon erected
and built with all Rights Previledges and / Appertinances to the same Premises or
any Part thereof / belonging or appertaining. To have & to hold the said One
Hundred Acres of Land and all and singular other the / before Bargained
Premises aforesd: and ev'ry Part and / Parcel thereof with their and ev'ry of their
Appertinances / together with the said Houses, Edifices & Buildings, thereupon
built unto the s[d]: WASSELL WEBLIN and GEORGE FADOINE and their

Heirs & Assigns forever Yeilding and paying thereof one Yearly / unto the Rent Gatherer for the publick Use, at the Feast of / S^t: Michael the Arch Angel his Fee Rent of Two shillings / And

[105]

And the s^d. JUSTINIAN COOPER and ANNE his Wife the s^d. 100 / Acres of Land, and Houses thereupon built and all and / singular other the Premises afores^d: and every Part and Parcel / thereof with the Appertinances, whatsoever, unto them the s^d: / WASSELL WEBLIN & GEORGE FADOINE and their Heirs against them / the s^d. JUSTINIAN COOPER and ANN his Wife, and their / Heirs, shall and will forever hereafter Warrant Defend / save, and keep harmless In Witness whereof the party's first / above named to these present Indentures, interchangably / have put their Hands & Seals [--] the day & Year first / above written

Signed Sealed & delivered   JUSTINIAN COOPER
In Presence of   ANNE COOPER
WILLIAM BARNARD JOHN WOULLF

Indorsed on the Backside of this Indenture the three / assignments following

Know all Men by these Presents That We WASSELL WEBLIN / and GEORGE FAWDON do Consign over and turn over our Right / Title of this Land forever unto ROBERT SABINE his Heirs Executors / and Administrators & Assigns forever that is specified on the / other Side at large Witness our Hands the 25th of February in / the Year of our Lord 1630

Witness   WASSELL WEBLING
WILLIAM BARNARD WILLIAM BUTLER   GEORGE FAWDON

Know all Man by these Presents That I ROBERT SABINE Doth / hereby Assign over unto CHRISTOPHER REYNOLDS of Warwicksqueak / all my Right to the aboves^d: CHRISTOPHER REYNOLDS all my Right / and

[106]

and Interest in the One Hundred Acres of Land expressed in the Bargain / of Sale, made unto WASSELL WEBLIN, and GEORGE FAWDON, from JUSTINIAN / COOPER and ANN COOPER his Wife, and I the said ROBERT SABINE / doth hereby surrender and deliver unto the s^d: REYNOLDS all my / Right and Interest in the same Witness my hand this 21st: of / December 1634

Witness by us   ꝓ me   ROBERT SABINE

ROBERT CRAMPORME
THOMAS COACHMAN

Know all Man That I CHRISTOPHER REYNOLDS for a Valuable /
Consideration to me paid by PETER HULL have Bargained and / Sold to the said
Peter his Heirs and Assigns forever all that / Parcel of Land within bargained &
Sold, by JUSTINIAN COOPER / and ANN his Wife to WASSELL WEBLING
& GEORGE FAWDON, and / by them sold to ROBERT SABINE and from him
to me the said CHRISTOPHER To have and to hold the said Land unto / the s^d.
PETER HULL his Heirs and Assigns forever and also all / Houses Edifices and
Buildings upon the same. And I the s^d: / CHRISTOPHER REYNOLDS Do
hereby Covenant and bind myself / and my Ex^rs and Assigns that the s^d: PETER
HULL his Heirs / and Assigns shall peaceable and Quietly Have Hold & Injoy
the / Premises and ev'ry Parcel thereof without any Trouble / Hindrance, or
Molestation of me the s^d: CHRISTOPHER, or the s^d: / ROBERT SABINE or our
heirs Ex^rs: or assigns or any other Person or / Persons that may have a Claim, any
Right Title or Estate in / the Premises or any Parcel thereof by from or under us
or any / of us. The s^d: CHRISTOPHER or ROBERT our Heirs or Assigns /
Witness my Hand the first day of May Anno 1639
Witness
JOHN SPACKMAN   CHRISTOPHER REYNOLDS
JOHN OLIVER

Examined & truly Transcribed / Test JA^S: BAKER Cl Cur

[107]
To all Christian People to whom these Presents shall / come I WILLIAM
YARRET of the Isle of Wight County in Virginia / Planter send Greeting in our
Lord God everlasting. Whereas Sir / FRANCIS WIAT late Governer, by Patent
under his Hand & Seal / of the Colony dated at James City the first Day of March
1640 / for the Consideration therein mentioned, Did Grant & Confirm / unto
HUGH WINN of the Isle of Wight County Planter his Heirs / and Assigns
forever Seven Hundred Acres of Land sicuate / lying and being within the
County afores^d: Upon & in the lower / Bay on the Western Side about two Mile
up the Bay and / Beginning at a marked White Oak standing at a Point at / Gut o
Valey by a small Island called Bennets Park [torn] / for Length West North Wes
Three Hundred and Twenty Pole / by and Adjoining on a Patent of Land o
SAMUEL JACKSON / to a marked Oak which standeth nigh a running Brook
and so running South: South: West Three Hundred & Fifty / Pole to a marked
Pine, which standeth at the Mouth of a / Creek called Goose Hill Creek, and so
running East South East / Three Hundred and Twenty Pole by a marked
Pohickory / along North: North: east Side of a Creek called Sewards / Creek to

the Utmost of the Mouth thereof and so running North / North: East. Three Hundred Fifty Pole, by the Bay Side to the / first mentioned White Oak standing Nigh to the Small Island / named Bennets Park, as by the s^d. Patent more at large may appear / And Whereas also the sd: HUGH WINN, by his Deed or Writing under / his Hand and Seal bearing Date the 21st: day of July Anno 1644 / for the Consideration therein also expressed Did Grant Bargain / Sell Confirme Assigne and Set over unto the s^d: WILLIAM YARRET my / my Heirs and Assigns forever three hundred & fifty Acres of / Land, being the full Moity of Half that of 750 Acres in the / afores^d. Patent mentioned to be granted as by the s^d: Deed or / Writing under the Hand of the s^d. HUGH WINN thereunto had / more

[108]

more at large may appear Now Know ye That I the said / WILLIAM YARRET for a Valuable Consideration in Hand received / at and before the Sealing hereof by THOMAS BRANDWOOD of / London Merchant well and truly satisfied and paid whereof / I do acknoledge the Receipt and thereof do acquit and hereby / Discharge the s^d: THOMAS BRANDWOOD his Heirs Ex^rs: and Adm^rs: and / every of them by these Presents Have Granted Confirmed Bargained / & Sold Assigned and Set over and by these Presents Do / fully clearly and absolutely Grant Confirm Bargain Sell / Assigne and set over unto him the said THOMAS BRANDWOOD / one Moity or half Part thereof of the s^d: 350 Acres of Land in the said / last recited Deed mentioned the same being in two Parts / equally devided together with one equal Moity or half / Part of all Houses Edifices or Buildings which now are / recited upon the same or any Part or Parcel thereof. / To have and to hold the said One Moity or half Part of / the s^d. Piece or Parcel of Ground before by these Presents / mentioned to be Bargained and Sold, with One Moity or half / Part of all Houses thereupon recited as afores^d: with all / mines & minerals therein contained, and all Rights of / Hunting Hawking Fishing and Fowling as also all Woods / Waters and River and all Hereditaments and / Commoditys whatsoever within the [--] of the s^d: Land / or any Part or Parcel thereof belonging or any Ways appertaining / unto the s^d. THOMAS BRANDWOOD his Heirs or assigns forever in / as large and ample Manner to all Intents & Purposes as in / the s^d Letters Patent or Deed before recited or either of them is / expressed he the s^d: THOMAS BRANDWOOD his Heirs or Assigns / paying all Quitrents as shall be due at any Time to his / Majesty his Heirs or Successors for the s^d. Lands As also yielding / and paying to his Majesty as afores^d: his due Share of all / Mines & Minerals mentioned in the s^d. Patent as aforesaid and / performing

[109]

performing all other Clauses which on his or their Parts, or / Behoof are or ought to be preformed, for the s^d: Moity of half / Party of 350 Acres of Land before by these Presents, bargained / and Sold. In Witness whereof I the s^d. WILLIAM YARRET have / hereunto set my Hand and Seal this 14th day of March Anno / 1646

Signed, Sealed & Delivered in psence of

RICH^D: WILLIAMSON Senr

THO^S: WOMBWELL

his

W^M: **8** YARRET the Seal

mark

Examined & Truly Transcribed / Teste JA^S: BAKER ClCur

This Indenture made the second Day / of April in the Twenty sixth Year of King Charles / Between AMBROS BENNET of the One Part and / RALPH WARRENER of the other Part Witnesseth / That the said AMBROS BENNET for a full and / valuable Consideration unto by the s^d: RALPH / well and truly paid before the Sealing hereof / hath Bargain'd Sold Assign'd and set over and / by these Presents Doth Bargain &c unto the said / RALPH WARRENER his heirs &c forever One / Hundred Acres of Land situated and being in / the County of Isle of Wight Part of a Dividend of / Eleven Hundred Acres of Land one to the s^d: / AMBROS by Patent Sign'd by the late Govern^r: / S^r: FRANCIS WIAT which s^d: Two hundred Acres / is bounded according as in the s^d: Patent / expressed bearing Date the twenty third of June / 1641 may appear and is the outmost Westerly / bounds

[110]
Bounds of theafores^d: Dividend of Eleven hundred / Acres lying between the Land of AMBROS / MEADER on the one Side and the Land of JOHN / MOTLEY and THOMAS TURNER on the other Side / part also of the s^d: dividend proportionably / bearing Length and Breadth according to the / s^d: Dividend To have, hold, and peaceably / Injoy the s^d: Two hundred Acres of Land with / all Previledges &c thereunto belonging and / warranting this to be a lawfull Deed of Sale / discharging and acquitting the s^d: RALPH / WARRENER his heirs &c from all former Bargains / Sales or Incumbrances whatsoever except the / Rents and Services one to the Kings most / excellent Majesty from henceforth to be paid / all Arrears of former Rents to be paid by the / s^d: AMBROS Lastly the s^d: AMBROS BENNET / Covenanteth that he and all other Persons / or any Time seized to his Use in the Premises / shall at all Times and Demands before the / seventh Day of April next coming suffer / or cause to be done and Suffered all and evry / such Thing and Things as shall tend to to [*sic*] the / further confirmation of this Sale unto the s^d: / RALPH WARRENER his heirs &c forever with / further Warranty against all Claims / Countermands or Opositions whatsoever / peaceably to injoy the Premises without any / Lett

Expullition or Eviction of the s^d: AMBROS / his heirs &c of any other persons by Reason / of any Title of Claim had or grown before / this

[111]
this Date In Witness of which Bargain / Sale and Grant on Behalf of the s^d: AMBROS / BENNET to be truly preformed he hath hereunto / set his Hand and Seal the Day and Year / above written
Sign'd Seal'd & Delivered   Signum
In Presence of   AMBROS **A** BENNET (Seal)
JAMES WILLIAMSON
THOMAS WOMBWELL

n. b. See the index of Court after the next following Deed

Examined and truly Transcribed / Teste JA^S BAKER

This Indenture made the seventh Day of / April in the twenty sixth Year of King Charles &c / Between AMBROS BENNET of the one Part and AMBROS / MEADER of the other Part Witnesseth That the s^d: AMBROS / BENNET for a full and valuable Consideration unto him / by the s^d: AMBROS MEADER well and truly paid before / the insealing hereof and hereby doth for himself his / Heirs &c acquit the s^d: AMBROS MEADER his Heirs &c Hath / Bargained and sold and by these Presents Doth / Bargain and sell unto the s^d: AMBROS MEADER his Heirs / &c forever Three Hundred acres of Land scituated in the / County the Isle of Wight, being part of a Dividend of / Eleven Hundred Acres due to the s^d: AMBROS BENNET by / Patent signed by S^r. FRANCIS WIAT late Govern^r: which s^d: / Three Hundred Acres is bounded as in the s^d: Patent / expressed, dated the 23^d. of June 1641 may Appear and is / the outmost Westerly bounds of the s^d: Dividend lying / betwixt the Land of CHRIST^r: REYNOLDS on the one Side and / RALPH

[112]
RALPH WARRENER on the other Side proportionably bearing / Length and Bredth, according to the s^d: Patent To have / hold and peaceably Injoy the s^d: three Hundred Acres of Land with all Priviledges &c thereunto belonging or / Warranting this t be a lawfull Deed of Sale discharging / and acquitting the s^d: AMBROS MEADER his Heirs &c from all / former Sales or Incumbrances whatsoever except the / Rent and Services due to the Kings most excellent / Majesty hence forward to be paid by the s^d: MEADER all / Arrears of former Rents to be paid by the s^d: BENNET. / Lastly the s^d: BENNET covenanteth that he and all other / Persons [--] seised to his Use in the Premises / shall at all

Demands before the seventh Day of April / next coming, cause or suffer to be done all such Things / as shall tend to the further Confirmation of this Sale unto / the s^d: MEADER his Heirs &c forever with further Warranty / against all Claims or Oppositions whatsoever / peaceably to injoy the Premises without the Lett / Expulsion or Eviction of the s^d: BENNET his Heirs &c / or any other persons by Reason of any Title had or Grown / before This Date. In Witness of which Sale and Grant / on the Behalf of the s^d: AMBROS BENNET to be well preformed / he hath hereunto set his Hand and Seal the Day and / Year above mentioned

Signed Sealed & Delivered   his
in Psence of   AMBROS **A** BENNET Siggillm:
JAMES WILLIAMSON   mark
THO^S: WOMBWELL

    The 9th: Day of June 1659. In open Court at the Isle of Wight / AMBROS BENNET Signed Sealed & delivered these Sales of Land unto / RALPH WARRENER & AMBROS MEADER according to the Contents / Test THOMAS WOMBWELL Cl: Cur: / Examined & truly Transcribed / Test JA^s: BAKER CCl

[113]
    In the Name of God. Amen. The seventh Day / of September 1694 [*sic*] I EDWARD CHETWINE of the Isle of Wight / County in Virginia being of weak State in Body but / sound in Mind and of perfect Memory do make / my last Will and Testament as followeth
    Imprimis I Bequeath my Soul to God my Creator, and my / Body to the Earth from whence it came and of the Goods / which God hath given me Imp^s I Give to JAMES HOUSE / & THOMAS ATTWELL one Year of their Times
    Item. I Give JAMES HOUSE all my Bedding and what else of / mine is at M^r. ALDREDs only one Brass [--] / my Boy THOMAS ATTWELL.
    Item I Give to CHRISTOPHER HOLMES all my wearing Apparrel
    Item. I Give JOHN YOUNG my Gun
    Item I Give M^r: / ROBERT WATSON HENRY PITT JOHN INGLISH NICHOLAS / ALDRED M^rs. ANNE JONES and all her Children each of / the afores^d. Partys one pair of Gloves and a Mourning / Bibbond [*sic*]
    Item to my Brother I Give my Lands Tenements and / Hereditaments with Thanks that he hath / supplied me notwithstanding he hither sent me / for a Sacrefise.
    And for the Preformance of this my Will & Testament / my Debts being paid I leave M^r. ROBERT WATSON and / HENRY PITT my Executors
    Probat^r: P Sacriment: THO^S. BROOK &

GULELMS RUFFIN 27° die Sep^r:1649   Nomen caret[12]

Examined and truly Transcribed / Test JA^S: BAKER ClCur

[114]
     In the Name of God. Amen. I JUSTINIAN COOPER / being sick and weak in Body, but of perfect memory do / make this my last Will and Testament as followeth. this / 26th of March 1650 Imprimis I Bequeath my Soul to God my Creator and mercifull Redeemer and my Body to / the Earth. I give and Bequeath my Estate as followeth / my Debts being paid I Give unto all my God children to / ev^{r}y one of them a Cow Calf a piece or so much Tob^o: / as shall buy them a Cow Calf to be paid the next insuing / Year I Give unto my Brother RICHARD COSSEY two Hundred / Acres of Land to him and his Heirs forever situate / lying and being the Land he and JOHN SNELLOCKE lives / on by the River Side and to be injoy'd by him and his / Heirs after my Wives Decease. I Give unto EDWARD PYLAND / Son of JAMES PYLAND five Hundred pounds Tob^o: to be paid / next Year which will be 1651. I make my loving wife / ANNE COOPER my true and lawfull Executrix of all / my Goods Lands Cattle Servants or whatsoever I am / possessed with, and I do likewise Request my loving / Friend Capt. WILLIAM BARNARD to be my overseer to see / this my Will performed and to take one or more to / himself to be an aid and assistant to my Wife whom / he shall think fit. I Give unto Capt. WILLM BARNARD a / piece of Plate of ten Pounds Price to be paid to him the / next year. 1651. And In Witness that this is my / last will and Testament I have hereunto set my Hand / and Seal the Day and Year first above written
Test JAMES PYLAND   JUSTINIAN **I C O** COOPER
JN^O: **IB** BRITT Signum

Examined and truly Transcribed / Test JA^S. BAKER Cl Cur

[115]
     This Indenture made the 5th: of Februy 1659. Between RICHARD YOUNG Planter of the one Part and ROBERT / PITT merchant of the other Part. Witnesseth That the said / RICHARD YOUNG hath clearly Bargained and Sole &c to the said / PITT his Patent of Land of 350 Acres lying upon New Town / Haven River between the Land of RICHARD PRESSON and / THOMAS JORDAN and in the like Manner hath sold One / Hundred Acres of Land as by Patent Granted by S^r. WILLIAM / BERKLEY Knight &c dated August 24th. 1648 which said / Land now in Occupation of WILLIAM DENSON and / JOHN ADDIS with all Appertinances &c due upon / the said Patent unto the s^d. PITT

---

[12] "The name is lacking."

77

and his Heirs &c / forever. Also the s^d. YOUNG hath sold all Writings, Receipts / &c which he or any Person hath in or concerning the / the [*sic*] Premises Covenanting to Deliver the same to the / s^d: PITT and in Consideration whereof the s^d: YOUNG / acknoledgeth to have Received full Content and / Payment by fifteen Hundred and Twenty Pounds / of Tob^o: of the s^d: PITT rece^d. And thereof acquits the sd. PITT / and his Heirs forever

Seal'd Sign'd & Delivered   Sign^m:
in Psense of   RICH^D: **R Y** YOUNG Siggillum
ROB^T: GAYLARD
ROBERT PITT Junr:

Examined and truly Transcribed / Tet [*sic*] / JA^S BAKER Cl Cur

NAME INDEX

Proper names are indexed according to the page numbers, in bars, of the original text. Numbers at the bottom of the page (of this *book*) have not been used as guides, only as pagination for the table of contents. Names may appear more than once on a page. An effort has been made to index females by their maiden and married names, and to distinguish males by their relationships to other persons or by their titles. The following items have not been indexed:

[1] Deities, names of monarchs and the countries over which they preside, or saints.
[2] Places or locations containing a proper name, such as "Seward's Swamp."
[3] The index to the text located on pp. 1-3 of this book.
[4] The chronological index to the text.
[5] Any information contained in the introduction.

[--]
(--) [m Dunster], 74
Alice [m Cranidge], 93
Ann [m1 Smith, 2 Bacon], 93
Ann [m Benn], 20
Ann [m Fawdon], 89
Ann [m1 Smith, 2 Fawdon], 92-93
Ann [m Watson], 29
Ann [m Williamson], 39
Anne [m1 Harrison, 2 Cooper], 94, 96,101-103,106,114
Anne [m Jones], 113
Annis [m Wilmouth], 19-20
Elizabeth [m Cobbs], 44,53-54
Elizabeth [m Brown], 85
Elizabeth [m King], 50
Elizabeth [m Reynolds], 47
Elizabeth [m Valentine], 31
Elizabeth [m Vasser], 30
Ellin [m Oliver], 80
Jane [m Clark], 70-71
John [w/o Jno], 38
Magdalin [m Barecroft], 90-91
Margaret [m1 Underwood, 2 Up-

ton], 32-33,39-42,62-65
Margaret [m1 Williamson, 2 Druett], 85-86
Margaret [m Yarrett], 55-57
Mary [m Motley], 79
Mary [m Watson], 69-70
Prudence [m1 Wilson, 2 Moon], 81 -84
Rebecca [m Bagnall], 12-13
Susannah [m Bird], 55-57

ABBOTT
Samuel, 3

ADDIS
John, 115

ALDRED
Nicholas, 88,113

ALLESON
George, 76

AMES
Richard, 30

ANDREWS
Willliam, 79

ARRAM
John, 27
John [s/o Jno], 27

ASKWE/ASKUE
John, 40,75-76

ATKINS
Richard, 52-53

ATTWELL
Thomas, 113

AYERS
Ffrancis, 61

BACON
Ann (--) Smith, 93
Nathaniel, 89,93

BAGNALL/BAGNELL
James, 13,38
Rebecca (--), 12-13
Roger, 12-13

BAKER
James, 1,3-5,7,9,11-15,17,19-21,23,
    25-27,29-30,32-34,37-38,
    40-44,46,48-51,53-54,56-
    57,60-61,65-66,68-70,72,
    74-80,85,87-90,92-94,96-
    97,99,101,106,109,111-115

BARCLY
J[ ], 89

BARECROFT/BARCROFT
Charles, 78,90-92
Magdalin (--) [w/o Chas], 90-91
William, 90-91

BARNARD
William [Capt.], 28,105,114

BARRY
David, 101

BATTS
John [Capt.], 40,62

BEAZLIE
Job, 92

BECKINO/BICKINOE
Edward, 78

BEDFORD
Peter, 69,78

BENN
Ann (--), 20
Christopher, 20-21

BENNETT
Alice (Peirce), 2-4,35
Ambrose, 21-23,33,39-40,79,
    109-112
Richard, 86
Richard [Gov.], 72
Robert, 95

BERKELEY
William [Gov.], 2,50,115

BERNARD
(--) [Col.], 28,77-78

BEUFORD
Anthony, 26

BILLINGSLY
John, 65

BIRD
Robert, 55-57,61,68,71,78,80
Susannah (--) [w/o Robt], 55-57

BOSTOCK
Alice, 72

BOSWELL
Thomas, 29

BOUCHER
Daniel, 1,28-29,53

BOZER
Andrew, 59

BRACEWELL
Robert [Rev.], 32,39

BRACEY/
BRASEE, see BRESSIE

BRADSHAW
Vincent, 63

BRANDWOOD
Thomas, 108

BRESSIE
Thomas, 26
William, 56-57,72

BREWER
James, 97
John, 51

BRICE
Thomas, 4-5

BRITT
John, 114
Robert, 115

BROOK
Thomas, 113

BROWN
Elizabeth (--) [w/o Geo], 85
George, 85

BRUNT
Jane, 71
William, 87

BULLEN
Sylvester, 48

BURGESS
John, 45-46

BURTON
John, 80

BUSH
Thomas, 34

BUTCHER
John, 40-41

BUTLER
John, 16
William, 105

BYHAM
Edward, 60

CARTER
John, 20
Thomas, 96

CAVALEIR
Isaac, 33

CHELD
John, 44

CHETWINE
Edward, 113

CHETWOOD
(--) [bro of Edw], 113
Edward, 26

CHIVERS
Thomas, 78

CLAPHAM
William, 10

CLARK
Humphrey, 38,61,68-70
Jane (--) [w/o Hum], 70-71
John [s/o Hum], 70-71
Mary, 71
Richard, 93

COACHMAN
Thomas, 106

COBBS
Benjamin, 44
Elizabeth [d/o Jos], 44
Elizabeth (--) [w/o Jos], 44,53-54
Joseph, 44
Pharoah, 44,53-54

COOPER
Ann (--) Harrison [m2 Cooper], 94,
96,101-103,106,114
Justinian, 2-3,6,76,78,94-96,101-
106,114

CORBOROFT
George, 20

CORDWENT
John, 54

CORSEY/COSSEY
Richard, 92,114

COSTARDE
John, 101

CRAMPORNE
Robert, 106

CRANIDGE
Alice (--) [m Js], 93
James, 93
William, 93

DARSON, see **DAWSON**

DAVIS
Thomas, 11-12,23-24,50,67

DAWSON/DARSON
William, 10-11,86

DEATH
Elizabeth [m Dodman], 17-18
Richard, 17-19
William, 18

DENBIGH
William, 76

DENSON
William, 115

DEWELL
Phillip, 41-42

DICKSON
Thomas, 1

DODMAN
Elizabeth (Death), 17-18
John, 17-19
John [Jr.], 18
Richard, 18

DODSON
Jarvase/Jarvaise, 57-60

DRAKE
James, 28

DRUETT
John, 85-86
Margaret (--) Williamson, 85-86

DUNN
Joseph, 44

DUNSTER
(--) [w/o Robt], 74
Leonard, 75
Robert, 29,74-75
William, 75

EGLESTON
Richard, 90

ELDRIDGE
Samuel, 68-69

ELLINGER
John, 14-15

ELMES
Thomas, 85-86

ELY
(--), 78
Robert, 98-99

ENGLAND
Ffrancis, 42-43,78,90

ENGLISH
John [Capt.], 63,65,113

**FFAWDON/FOWDEN/
FADOINE**
Ann (Smith) [w/o Geo], 89,92-93
George, 5,39,88-89,92-93,96,103-
106

FENN
[child], 1

[dau.], 1
[son], 1
[wife], 1
Timothy, 1

FLAKE
Robert, 68

FLINTON
Farrar, 100-101

FLUELLEN
[dau.], 29
Thomas, 29

FREESTONE
Henry, 22

FULGHAM
Anthony, 67

GARLAND
Joan/John [m Wilson], 83
Peter, 84
Prudence (--) [m2 Wilson, 3 Moon],
    81-84

GATLIN
John, 40

GARRETT
Edward, 4

GAYLARD
Robert, 115

GELLIE
George, 1

GEORGE
Isaac [s/o Jno], 88-89
John [Major], 28,88-89,94-96
Nicholas, 61,76-77

GODWIN
William, 71

GORDONE
Thomas, 54

GRAVES
Robert, 60

GREENWOOD
Thomas, 6,8-9

GRIMES
Eustace, 53

GUTTERIDGE/GOODRICH
John, 90

GYAR/GYER
Robert, 15
Thomas, 16-17

GYLES
John, 100

HAMER
Raphe [Capt.], 101

HAMMOND
John,97

HARDING
[--], 35

HARDY
George, 97

HARRIS
Robert, 17
Thomas, 57-60

HARRISON/HARRIS
Anne (--) [m2 Cooper], 94,96,101-
      103,106,114
James, 101,103

HARST
Toby, 29

HARVEY
George [Gov.], 102
John [Gov.], 23,32,65-66

HASWELL
Samuel, 53-54

HAWKES
(--), 57

HAWKINS
John, 75-76

HAWOOD
Thomas, 24

HIGGENS
Ffrancis, 45,49

HILL
Nicholas [Major], 77-78
Thomas, 65-66

HINSON
Thomas, 87

HOBBS
Francis [Capt.], 14-15,58-60

HOLMES
Christopher, 113
Thomas, 71-72

HOLT
Thomas, 12

HOUSE
James, 113

HOW
Jane, 71

HOWELL
Hopkin, 22-23

HULL
Peter, 69,106

INGLAND, see **ENGLAND**

INNES
James, 66

IZARD
Richard, 63

JACKSON
John, 20
Mary [d/o Rich], 4
Richard, 4
Samuel, 107
Sarah [d/o Rich], 4

JAKINS
James, 90

JENNINGS
Owen, 84

JEWRY
William, 26-27

JOHNSON
Elizabeth [goddau/o John Stiles], 37
Henry, 99
Thomas, 37

JONES
Anne (--), 113
Anthony, 5,25-26,69,99-100
Catharine [sist/Anth], 25
Gyles/Giles, 101-104
Nathaniel, 67
Thomas, 21,67
William [bro/Anth], 25

JORDAN
Richard, 46,93-94,100
Thomas, 115

JUX
William, 75

KAE/KEA
Robert, 66,78

KEERKE
Thomas, 87-88

KEMP
Richard [Gov.], 35-36,66

KING
Elizabeth (--) [w/o Jno], 50
John, 38,50,63

KNIGHT
Peter, 7,9,24,65-66

LAMBERT
Francis, 14-15

LACEY
William, 15-16

LAWRENCE/LAURENCE
Gyles, 63
Robert, 35-36,78

LAWSON
[ ], 16

LEE
Hugh, 93
Richard, 12

LEWER
William, 49,86

LEWIS/LEWES
Christopher, 45-46,90
John, 30
Thomas, 61,78
William, 31,34,100

LOBB
George, 51,93-94

LOCKYER
Richard, 29

MADDIN
Joane [goddau/o Jno Stiles], 37

MADDISON
Richard, 67

MARSHALL
John, 31

MATHEWS
Anthony, 48,94
Sam, 29

MEADOR
Ambrose, 11,110-112

MOON
John [Capt.], 24,67,81
Mary [d/o Jno], 81-84
Prudence (--) Wilson, 81-84
Sara [d/o Jno], 81-84
Susannah [d/o Jno], 81-84

MOORE/MOORES
George, 92
Henry, 79

MORRIS
Nicholas, 38

MOSELEY
William, 42

MOTLEY/MOTLY
John, 21-22,33-34,79,110
Mary (--) [w/o Jno], 79

MUNGER
John, 1

MURRY
John [godsn/o Jno Stiles], 37

NEAL
Christopher, 18
Daniel, 18

NETHERCOAT
Nicholas, 32

NEWMAN
John, 101

NEWTON
John, 87

NICHOLAS
John ,76-77

NICHOLS/NICHOLES
Samuel, 34,81

OLIVER
[dau.], 80
[dau.], 80
Ellin (--) [w/o Jno], 80
John, 5-8,79-80,92,106
John [s/o Jno], 80

PAIGE
Joseph, 103

PARKER
Thomas, 25

PARKES
Robert, 53

PARRY
Phillip, 88

PARTIN
Robert, 13-14

PAWLEY
John, 28-29,52-53,78

PAYNE
John, 14

PEARCE
(--) [Capt.], 43

PEIRCE
Alice [m Bennett], 2-4,35

PENNY
Elizabeth, 27
Richard, 27

PETTEFER
William, 76

PEVERAL
John, 29

PITT
Henry, 4-5,69-70,113
Richard, 87
Robert, 115
Robert [Jr.], 115

PLAISE
Francis, 95

POOL
Thomas, 63

POWELL
Howell, 58,77

Thomas, 77

PRESSON
Richard, 115

PRICE
Robert, 23

PRINCE
Edward, 78,97

PRITCHARD
Thomas, 51

PRYME
Edward, 78

PYLAND
Edward [s/o Js], 114
James, 4,7,9,29-30,36,38,43,45-46,
        51,80,114

RAWLES
George, 23

REINING
John, 80

REYNOLDS
Abbasha [d/o Chr], 47
Christopher, 46-47,105-106,111
Elizabeth [d/o Chr], 47
Elizabeth (--) [w/o Chr], 47
Jane [d/o Chr], 47
John [s/o Chr], 46-47
Richard [s/o Chr], 47

RIVERS
George, 47

ROCHE
James, 4-5

RUFFIN
Robert, 27
William, 27,79,113

SABIN/SABINE
Robert, 36,105-106

SCOTT
Thomas, 33

SEWARD
John, 13-14,76,87

SHARP
John, 58
Richard, 46,94

SHERY
John, 71

SKINNER/SKYNNER
Edward, 40-42,68
Arthur, 79

SLAUGHTER
Ffrancis, 62-65

SMARLEY
William, 99-100

SMITH
Ann (--) [m2 Bacon], 93
Ann [d/law of Antho Jones], 25
Ann [m Fawdon], 92-93
John, 6,16,26,51
Richard, 74
Thomas, 26
William [bro/o Fawdon], 93

SNELLOCK
John, 77-78,100-101,114

SPACKMAN
John, 72,106

SPARKS
John, 41,69

STAMPE/STAMP
Thomas, 28,52

STEPHENS
George, 29,97

STILES
Elizabeth (--) [w/o Jno], 38
John, 37-38
John [s/o Jno], 37

STEWART
Charles, 13

SWEET
John, 42-43

SYLLIVANT
Dennis, 82

SYMONS
(---), 40

SYMPSON
John, 73-74

TABERER
Josuath/Joshua, 48-49
Ruth [d/o Tho], 49
Thomas [br/o Josh], 45,48-49,61,78
William [father of Josh], 48
William [br/o Josh], 48

TAYLOR
James, 3,39-41

THACKER
William, 57,59-60

THATCHER
Sylvester, 67-68

TOMLIN
John, 67

TOOKE
James, 15-17

TRAVERS
William, 75

TROLODER
William, 98-99

TURNER
Thomas, 21-22,33-34,79,110

UNDERWOOD
Elizabeth [d/o Margaret], 39
Margaret [d/o Margaret], 39
Margaret (--) [m2 Upton], 32-33,39-
    42,62-65
Sarah [d/o Margaret], 39
William [s/o Margaret], 32-34,38-40

UPTON
John [Capt., Lt.-Col.], 5-11,20-
    21,32-34,38,40-42,62-63,65
John [s/o Jno], 38
Margaret (--) Underwood, 32-33,39-
    42,62-65

VALENTINE/VALLENTINE
Ann [d/o Jno], 31-32

Elizabeth [d/o Jno], 31
Elizabeth [w/o Jno], 31
James [s/o Jno], 31
John, 30,32,34
Margaret [d/o Jno], 31

VASSER
Ann [d/o Jno], 30
Elizabeth [d/o Jno], 30
Elizabeth [w/o Jno], 30
John, 30
John [s/o Jno], 30
Mildred [d/o Jno], 30
Peter [s/o Jno], 30

WALTER
Thomas, 30,69

WARD
Lawrence, 50,63

WARNER
Thomas, 46

WARRENER
Ralph, 109-112

WARRINGE
William, 99

WASHBORN
Daniel, 36

WATKINS
John, 97

WATTS
Henry, 72-74,81

WATSON
Ann (--) [wid/Robt], 29,
James [bro/Robt], 29,41,69-70,87
John [bro/Robt], 29
Mary [w/o Js], 69-70
Robert, 26,29,69,88,113

WATTON
Thomas, 99

WAY
Richard, 67

WEBB
Elizabeth, 75
Stephen, 97
Thomas, 53

WEBBLING
Wassell/Wessell, 103-106

WEEKS
Joseph, 13-14

WELLS
St. Mount/Tantemount, 78,89

WESTRAY
William, 19,27,32,74

WHITAKER
William, 99

WHITE
Henry, 28-29,53
John, 11

WICKENS
Edmond, 78

WHITTINGTON
Francis, 34

WIAT, see **WYATT**

WILLIAMS
John, 71
John [Welchman], 71
Richard, 92

WILLIAMSON
Ann (--) [w/o James], 39
Margaret (--) [m2 Druett], 85-86
James, 11,39,111-112
Richard, 21,34,41,85,101,109

WILMOUTH/WILMOT
Annis (--), 19-20
Edward, 19-20,28-29
Frances, 19
John, 19
Robert, 19

WILSON/WILLSON
Joan/John (Garland) [d/o Pru], 83
Prudence (--) [m2 Moon], 81-84
William [s/o Pru], 83

WINCHELL
Robert, 99-100

WINN
Hugh, 55-57,107

WOMBWELL
Thomas, 5,11,17,24-25,109,111-112

WOOD
Arthur, 99

WOODROSE
Robert, 17

WOODWARD
Thomas, 43,56-57,65,70,77,79,
    87,93

WOULF
John, 105

WRIGHT
Thomas, 75

WYATT
Francis [Gov.], 22,107,109,111

YARRETT
Margaret (--) [w/o Wm], 55-57
William, 55-57,107-109

YOUNG
John, 113
Richard, 115

PLACE INDEX

Every conceivable name indicating a place or location, formal or informal, real or implied, has been indexed. Places may appear more than once on each page, and the index is keyed to the actual pages of the original text, not the pages of this book. The following items will not appear in this index:

[1] The first three pages of this book (pp. 1-3).
[2] The re-constituted chronological arrangement of the instruments within.
[3] Names of countries or colonies over which monarchs and governors preside.
[4] Any information contained in the introduction.

Goose Hill, 44
Main, 102,104
Quarter, 95

MILLS, etc.
(--), 52
Mill Dam, 78
Water, 97

MISCELLANEOUS PLACES
Bachelors Plantation, 65
Barrens, 68
Burying Place,74
King of all Places, 82
Landing Place, 20
Mansion house of Gyles Jones, 102,
   104
Plantation of Mr. Lawson, 16
Stanley Hundred, 51
Stockers, 2
Turkey Hill, 50
Valley, 107

NECKS
(--), 13,28
Poplar, 82
Rowlands, 40

POINTS
Piney, 20
Red, 23,82
Upper Red, 11

WOODS
(--), 6,10,23,28,45,65,73,92,95
Main, 6,12,57,63

PREVIOUS PUBLICATIONS

"The Maternal Ancestry of Gov. Augustus Hill Garland," in *The Arkansas Family Historian*, vol. 17, no. 1 [Jan-Mar 1979], pp. 25-27.[1]

"Wilkinsons of Virginia and Yazoo County, Mississippi," in *The Virginia Genealogist*, vol. 24, no. 4 [Oct-Dec 1980], pp. 178-80.

"Almost *Mayflower* Descendants in the Carolinas," in *Nexus*, vol. 8, no. 1 [Feb-Mar 1991], pp. 24-25.

"Following the Clues: The Family of Dr. Joel Walker," in *Tennessee Ancestors*, vol. 7, no. 1 [Apr 1991], pp. 55-59.

"The Ancestry of Tennessee Williams," in *Nexus*, vol. 8, nos. 3 & 4 [June-Aug 1991], pp. 108-112.

"The Maternal Ancestry of Henry Soane," in *The Virginia Genealogist*, vol. 35, no. 3 [July-Sept 1991], pp. 163-72.

"The Ancestry of Tennessee Williams," in *Tennessee Ancestors*, vol. 7, no. 2 [Aug 1991], pp. 159-204.

"The Descendants of Moses White of Rowan Co., NC," in *Tennessee Ancestors*, vol. 7, no. 3 [Dec 1991], pp. 303-66.

"Carter, Helms, and Presley--A Foray into the Piedmont *Non-Plantation South*," in *Nexus*, vol. 8, no. 6 [Dec 1991], pp. 204-06.

"Using Middle Names To Establish a *Burned County* Pedigree," in *The Virginia Genealogist*, vol. 36, no. 3 [July-Sept 1992], pp. 163-72.

A series of articles (concerning the English ancestry of the following families: Castlyn, Fisher, Knapp, Lake, Lucas, Oldham, Sowter, Whitman), in John Brooks Threlfall, *Twenty-Six Great Migration Colonists to New England and Their Origins*. Madison, Wis., 1993.

---

[1] A work of extreme youth which should be treated with extreme caution.

"Hollywood Gothic and the Alabama Three," in *Nexus*, vol. 10, no. 4 [Aug-Sept 1993], pp. 110-15.

The Complete Ancestry of Tennessee Williams. Jackson, Miss., 1993.

"An Illegitimate and a 'Legitimate' Royal Descent for John Fisher of Virginia," in *The Virginia Genealogist*, vol. 38, no. 4 [Oct-Dec 1994], pp. 283-89.

An Addendum to The Complete Ancestry of Tennessee Williams: *The Ancestry of Gen. James Robertson, "Father of Tennessee."* Jackson, Miss., 1995.

The Five Thomas Harrises of Isle of Wight County, Virginia. Jackson, Miss., 1995.[2]

"A Royal Descent for Christopher Calthorpe of York Co., VA," in *The Virginia Genealogist*, vol. 40, no. 1 [Jan-Mar 1996], pp. 64-67.

The Descendants of Cheney Boyce, "Ancient Planter," and of Richard Craven, for Seven Generations. Jackson, Miss., 1996.

"Joseph Bridger of Dursley, Gloucestershire," in *The Virginia Genealogist*, vol. 41, no. 3 [July-September, 1997], pp. 183-84.

"Subtle Recognition in Seventeenth-Century Virginia," in *The American Genealogist*, vol. 73, no. 1 [Jan 1998], p. 10.

"The Batte Family of Birstall, Yorkshire, and Bristol Parish, Virginia," in *The Virginia Genealogist*, vol. 42, no. 3 [July-September, 1998], pp. 214-30.

"William[3] Tooke's Children: A Reinvestigation," in *The Virginia Genealogist*, vol. 42, no. 4 [October-December, 1998], pp. 291-99.

Colonial Families of Surry and Isle of Wight Counties, Virginia. Vol. 2 *The Descendants of Robert Harris*. Jackson, Miss., 1999.

---

[2] This is actually the first volume of *Colonial Families of Surry and of Isle of Wight Counties, Virginia*.

"The Will of Arthur Jones of Bermuda," in *The Virginia Genealogist*, vol. 43, no. 3 [July-September, 1999], pp. 227-31.

"Of Things Clerical," in *Friends of the Virginia State Archives, Archives News*, vol. 9, no. 2 [Fall 1999], pp. 1 and 12.

Colonial Families of Surry and Isle of Wight Counties, Virginia. Vol. 3, *Isle of Wight Co., VA, Court Orders, Oct 1693-May 1695.* Jackson, Miss., 1999.

In collaboration with Kenneth W. Kirkpatrick, "Cottoniana, or 'That Cotton-Pickin' Somerby!' ", in *The New Hampshire Genealogical Record*, vol. 16, no. 4 [Oct 1999], pp. 145-70.

"*By a Line of Marked Trees,*" *Abstracts of Currituck Co., NC, Deed Books [1], 1-2, and 3, pp. 1-122.* Jackson, Miss., 2000.

"The Ancestry of Robert Batte," in *The Virginia Genealogist*, vol. 44, no. 3 [July-September, 2000], pp. 163-71.

"America's Best Southern Genealogical Libraries," in *Friends of the Virginia State Archives, Archives News*, vol. 10, no. 2 [Fall 2000], pp. 1, 4-7.

"The Ancestry of Robert Batte (concluded)" in *The Virginia Genealogist*, vol. 44, no. 4 [October-December 2000], pp. 301-08.

"The Ancestry of Thomas Cullen," in *The North Carolina Genealogical Journal*, vol. 26, no. 4 [Nov 2000], pp. 363-75.

"Madam Ester Pollock and the Cullens," in *The North Carolina Genealogical Journal*, vol. 26, no. 4 [Nov 2000], pp. 376-92.

"The Ancestry of Edward Jones of Isle of Wight County, Virginia," in *The Virginia Genealogist*, vol. 45, no. 1 [January-March, 2001], pp. 66-70.

Colonial Families of Surry and Isle of Wight Counties, Virginia. Vol. 4, *The Descendants of Capt. John Jenings of Isle of Wight Co., VA.* Jackson, Miss., 2001.

www.ingramcontent.com/pod-product-compliance
Lightning Source LLC
Chambersburg PA
CBHW070255290326
41930CB00041B/2555